More Things I Wish I'd Known

Various contributors
Edited by Michelle Gant

Copyright © 2025 Michelle Gant
All rights reserved
ISBN: 9798309102235
Imprint: Independently published

Cover design by Christina Leigh

For Jenny Playford, who taught me so much of what I know now, and especially what it means to be a great mother, which she truly was.

Thank you

I do not underestimate what a thing it is to write down and share your innermost thoughts, your personal experiences, your feelings so openly and vulnerably. So, my heartfelt thanks must go to these amazing women who have shared their stories within these pages. Thank you to:

Claire Staddon, Gemma Brown, Hannah Freeman, Georgina Phillips, Jana Patey, Katie Faulkner, Lisa Collen, Lisa Dymond, LJ, Lorna Blackmore, Luisa Stanney, Marie Connell, Philippa Sillis, Rebecca Price, Sam James, Sarah Gill, Sauy Li, Sharon Clifton, Steph Allen, Suzanne Thompson, and Vicki Haverson.

And thank you to everyone who has supported this project and this book.

Michelle Gant, January 2025

Contents

Introduction	9 - 11
My body, my voice, my worth Lorna Blackmore	12 - 18
Running is not for everyone Philippa Sillis	19 - 23
Fear became my superpower Michelle Gant	24 - 31
A thing learnt along the way: Take another look	32
Embracing my uniqueness Gemma Brown	33 - 35
A thing learnt along the way: We rise by lifting others	36 - 37
Lessons in friendship Sauy Li	38 - 39
A thing learnt along the way: There is magic in the ordinary	40 - 41
Living by my values Sarah Gill	42 – 48

A thing learnt along the way: 49 - 50
     In this moment, all is well

Accepting grief   51 - 53
     Marie Connell

The older I get the less I know   54 - 56
     Claire Staddon

A thing learnt along the way: 57 - 58
     We don't have to have all the answers

How will you know if you don't try?   59 - 62
     Sharon Clifton

Make time to talk   63 - 67
     Steph Allen

A thing learnt along the way: 68
     Listening is an act of love

It's ok to be you   69 - 72
(however that looks)
     Luisa Stanney

A thing learnt along the way: 73 - 74
     Life is life

Life can change in an instant   75 - 82
     and you only get one shot; make it count
     LJ

A thing learnt along the way: 83
    There is always hope, there is always help

Follow your own path 84 - 88
    and not the path of expectations
    Sam James

Know your purpose, 89 - 90
    trust your instincts, and stay present
    Lisa Collen

A thing learnt along the way: 91 - 92
    Small steps will help you travel far

Find who you've always been 93 - 96
    Rebecca Price

What the menopause 97 - 104
    has taught me
    Vicki Haverson

A thing learnt along the way: 105
    Find the source of your power

You need to slam a few doors 106 - 107
    Suzanne Thompson

When to apologise 108 - 115
    Lisa Dymond

A thing learnt along the way: Leave some blank space	116 - 117
If it matters to you, it matters Hannah Freeman	118 - 122
Navigating work and motherhood Jana Patey	123 - 130
Time is our most precious commodity Katie Faulkner	131 - 138
A thing learnt along the way: There's time and then there's what you do with it	139 - 140
Prioritise what matters to you Georgina Phillips	141 - 144
Don't ignore what burns inside Michelle Gant	145 - 150
A thing learnt along the way: Choose your own story	151
References	152
Keep in touch	153
Your space	154 - 166

Introduction

"Every woman's success should be an inspiration to another. We're strongest when we cheer each other on," – Serena Williams.

We live in a world that routinely pits women against each other. For the choices we make, the way we look, the things that we do, the words that we say. We are constantly told that we're not enough, that we're too much. We are judged if we do, and we're judged if we don't.

But the truth is that we are sisters, not rivals.

And this could not be truer than within the pages of this book. Here you will find the reflections, the thoughts, the personal experiences of women who are sharing what they have learnt along the way. Openly, honestly, vulnerably. Women of different ages and backgrounds who have come together to talk about the things they wish they had known. I hope that within these essays you may find something that interests, inspires, or connects with you.

Throughout the book, you'll also find some snapshots of practical ideas and experiences - things learnt along the way.

Our commitment to supporting other women goes beyond what's written here – all the royalties from this book will go to Women's Aid. By buying this book, you are making a difference.

This is the second volume of the Things I Wish I'd Known. These books originally came about because a few years ago I looked at my daughter and thought: there are so many things I want you to know. That idea evolved into these books, made possible by the amazing contributors who have added their voices.

The first book – published in 2023 – was created with my thoughts focused on the next generation of girls, on lifting them up, and helping them to thrive. This time however, as I've edited this collection, my mind has been very much on the women who went before us, the women who created and cleared the path that we now follow.

And so, a huge note of gratitude to all those women – our mothers, grandmothers, aunties, our female ancestors, and many, many more women we have never met – who have done the groundwork so that we can live the lives that we do today. The women who have passed on their learning to us, or who have taken a stand for our rights, or who have been at the forefront of making changes that benefit women today.

We stand on the shoulders of giants.

I really hope you enjoy More Things I Wish I'd Known, and if you want to capture your own reflections, there's space at the end to do just that.

Michelle Gant, January 2025

My body, my voice, my worth
Lorna Blackmore

Growing up as a woman in a world that constantly bombards us with images of 'perfection' is no easy feat. Looking back, there are so many things I wish I had known about my body, about beauty, and about self-worth that could have saved me from years of doubt, insecurity, and needless comparison. If I could go back and talk to my younger self—or to any young woman—these are the truths I would share.

1. Your body is a work in progress
One of the most important lessons I've learned is that our bodies are constantly evolving. As a teenager, the dawning of curves was not a welcome change for me. I struggled to reconcile this shift with how I thought I should look, and it led me down a difficult path, eventually triggering an eating disorder. I wish I had known then that puberty and its changes are natural and not something to fight against.

Our bodies are not static; they change with time, experiences, and circumstances like pregnancy, stress, or ageing. I've come to understand that no one has a 'perfect' body and that these changes are part of life's journey. If I could go back, I'd remind myself to treat my body with kindness and patience, understanding that every stage is valid and beautiful in its own way.

2. You're more than what you look like

As a society, we tend to focus too much on how women look rather than who they are. Growing up, I spent countless hours scrutinising my appearance, obsessing over whether I was 'pretty enough.' But as I've grown older, I've realised that our value as women isn't determined by a reflection in the mirror. What truly defines us is our kindness, intelligence, strength, and the way we treat others.

From a mixed heritage, I often felt self-conscious about looking 'different' and not fitting neatly into one cultural beauty standard. I wish I'd known to celebrate my unique features and the rich diversity they represent, rather than trying to blend in. Embracing your heritage and how it shapes your appearance can be a powerful reminder that beauty is multifaceted, and your individuality is your strength.

3. The media lies about beauty

From a young age, we're exposed to idealised images of beauty that are carefully curated, airbrushed, and filtered. These images can create an impossible standard, leaving many women feeling inadequate. What I didn't know then is that even the models in those photos don't look like that in real life. I wish I had understood that beauty comes in all shapes, sizes, and colours, and that the media's version of beauty is neither realistic nor attainable for most people. Real beauty is diverse and imperfect - and that's what makes it so compelling. Everyone has insecurities, even those who seem 'perfect' to you, so focus on celebrating your unique qualities. There's no one else in the world quite like you, and that's something to be proud of.

4. Diet culture is toxic

What I've learned is that health isn't about being a certain size or following a restrictive diet. Having always been conscious of my weight, I often felt the pressure to monitor every bite, even though I've never been overweight. Despite being healthy, I internalised the belief that I needed to be thinner to be 'enough,' a mindset reinforced by societal ideals.

What I've learned is that health isn't about being a certain size or adhering to restrictive diets. It's about nourishing your body, moving in ways that feel good, and taking care of both your physical and mental wellbeing. The idea that you have to earn your food or feel guilt of overindulging is harmful and untrue. Food is fuel, and your worth isn't measured by the number on a scale. Recognising this has been a transformative step in healing my relationship with my body.

5. It's okay to take up space

As women, we're often taught to shrink ourselves— not just physically, but emotionally and intellectually. I wish I'd known that it's okay to take up space, to speak your mind, and to demand respect. This applies to body image, too. You don't need to apologise for your size, your shape, or your presence. Confidence isn't about fitting into a mould; it's about owning who you are and showing up unapologetically. It starts when you stop seeking permission to be yourself.

6. Exercise should be a celebration, not a punishment

For years, I saw exercise as a way to 'fix' my body. It felt like something I had to do to make up for eating or to achieve a specific look. I wish I'd known that movement can—and should—be joyful. Whether it's running, cycling, dancing, hiking, weights, or yoga, finding activities you love transforms exercise from a punishment into a celebration of what your body can do.

Beyond the physical benefits, exercise is also incredibly powerful for the mind. Moving your body releases endorphins, which can help lift your mood, reduce stress, and even ease symptoms of anxiety and depression. For me, it's become a form of therapy, a chance to clear my head and reconnect with myself. The more I focus on how exercise can make me feel, the more I came to appreciate it as an act of self-care, not self-control.

7. Clothing sizes don't define you

How often have you let the number on a clothing tag dictate your mood? I wish I'd known that sizes are arbitrary and vary wildly between brands and countries. A size is just a number - it doesn't reflect your worth, your beauty, or your health. Wear what makes you feel comfortable, beautiful, and confident, regardless of the label.

8. Speak kindly to yourself
The way we talk to ourselves matters. I used to be my harshest critic, constantly focusing on my perceived flaws. Over time, I've realised that negative self-talk only perpetuates insecurity. I wish I'd started practicing self-compassion earlier, reminding myself that I'm deserving of love and acceptance, just as I am. Treating yourself with kindness is one of the most powerful ways to improve your relationship with your mind and body.

9. The people who love you, love you for you
When I was younger, I often worried about how others saw me. Did they notice my flaws? Did they think I was too big or too small? As I've grown older, I've come to realise that the people who truly love you don't care about those things. They see your heart, your personality, and your unique qualities. I wish I'd spent less time worrying about impressing others and more time embracing the love and acceptance I already had.

10. Ageing is a privilege
As women, we're often made to feel like ageing is something to fear. The pressure to look young

forever is intense, but it's also unrealistic. I wish I'd understood sooner that ageing is a privilege denied to many. Wrinkles, grey hair, and other signs of ageing are proof that we've lived, experienced, and grown.

11. Confidence is the most attractive thing you can wear

It sounds cliché, but it's true: confidence makes you shine. No matter your size, shape, or style, the way you carry yourself can transform how others see you. I wish I'd known that self-assurance is more powerful than any makeup, outfit, or diet. When you believe in your own worth, others will too.

I've also come to realise the importance of respecting and recognising the wisdom, resilience, and stories age gives us. Society often marginalises older women, but, valuing experience reminds us that ageing is not a decline - it's an accumulation of beauty, courage, and knowledge that deserves honour and respect.

12. Surround yourself with positivity

The people and messages we surround ourselves with have a significant impact on how we see ourselves. I wish I'd been more mindful of this earlier, avoiding toxic relationships and negative influences. Seek out friends, mentors, and communities that uplift and empower you. Follow social media accounts that celebrate diversity and body positivity. The more positivity you invite into your life, the easier it becomes to love yourself.

13. Self-acceptance takes time—and that's okay
Finally, I wish I'd known that self-acceptance is a journey, not a destination. It's okay to have days when you don't feel your best. What matters is that you keep moving forward, learning to embrace yourself a little more each day. Growth takes time, and every step you take is worth celebrating.

Looking back, I wish I'd had the wisdom and perspective I have now. If there's one thing I want every woman to know, it's that you are enough—just as you are. Your worth isn't tied to your appearance, and your beauty isn't defined by anyone else's standards.

Embrace your uniqueness, celebrate your strengths, and remember: you are so much more than what the world sees.

Running is not for everyone
Philippa Sillis

When I was about six, my mother thought that I seemed bright so she decided to have my intelligence tested.

(Don't ask.)

While the type of intelligence testing that was standard in the 1970s has subsequently been widely (and rightly) condemned, the result I achieved led to a belief in our family that I was 'very clever'.

I was joined up as a member of the National Association for Gifted Children. I was put up a year at school.

I, too, bought into this belief and thought that I must be 'very clever'.

Whether through the weight of my own expectations or those of others, I developed the idea over time that this also meant I should be 'very good at everything'. I was the type of person who would grow up to change the world.

I must be very good at academic learning. I must be very good at playing an instrument. I must be very good at sport. I must be very good at anything I try to do.

Although crucially, I will not actually have to try at any of these things. Trying will not be necessary because I am very good at everything.

However, a technical hitch that was probably not a surprise to anyone except me arose with this thinking. As I started to experience more of the world around me, I started to see that I am not very good at a lot of things.

By the time I got to secondary school I began to discover that academic success would not be won without some effort.

Progress on the piano would require practice. I can only imagine what I put my mother through as I sawed ungracefully on my cello.

And then there was running.

I am not good AT ALL at running. Cross-country running would see me trailing miserably at the back. Sprinting was nothing less than a mortification.

I can't say I exactly put my back into it – that would be trying, which was not on.

And it's not that I didn't enjoy sport at all – I loved playing tennis throughout my childhood and hockey at secondary school.

But really, running defeated me. It made my chest heave, turned my face an unflattering shade of red and made my legs feel as if they had diving weights attached. (All of this still applies).

This is not good for the confidence of the person who thinks there is an expectation of them being 'very good at everything'.

My immature emotions did not cope at all well with these hitches. As time went by my attainment at school at school disintegrated. I left school with mediocre GCSEs, I left college with (after three attempts) mediocre 'A' levels, and university with a mediocre degree.

I did not continue with the piano or, probably to the relief of anyone who ever heard me play, the cello.

Yet for some reason I could not entirely let go of running.

Goddamn it I SHOULD be able to do it!

Over the years I have given it a go a number of times. Sometimes on my own, sometimes with the help of a programme such as Couch-to-5k. I've tried running on the treadmill at the gym to get me started.

At times, I came dangerously close to putting some effort into this endeavour.

Worse still, my efforts were not always undertaken where failure could be dealt with in private.

A few years ago I rashly agreed to take part in the mothers' race at sports day. I painfully strained my quadriceps from the shock to these unstretched muscles, while also suffering the humiliation of being overtaken by someone whose boot had fallen off on the start line and she'd had time to stop to put it back on.

Running has not been good for me, or kind to me.

Meanwhile, a combination of honest self-reflection and life experience has taught me that I am not 'very clever'. There are lots of things I'm good at and there are some things I'm really good at. There are lots of things I'm not good at and there are some things I'm really terrible at. And the world at large really doesn't care that much anyway.

On balance, while I find it can be really hard to break yourself of some of your formative ideas I think I'm learning to make peace with myself.

Developing an interest in astronomy has helped. Seeing how very small I am in the grand scheme of things helps me to put things in perspective.

If I want to do something, I might not know much about it and I might not be very good to start with.

But that's okay. I can try, I can practice, I can get better.

My ambitions have changed. I no longer dream of changing the world, I just hope that when my time is up the tiny imprint of my life on it is one that has done more good than harm.

Letting go of some of the weight has enabled me to start thinking less about what I 'should' be like and more about what I 'am' like. Part of this is learning about what I like.

And this brought to me a revelation.

I hate running.

I really, really hate running. I do not enjoy it, I have never enjoyed it. And crucially, whether I am any good at it or not is irrelevant. It does not have an adverse effect on anyone if I don't run so if I don't enjoy it, I don't have to do it. And THAT'S OKAY.

So I'll stick to walking my dog, baking, learning about the stars, reading, and spending time with people I love.

These are things I like.

No more running. Running is not for everyone.

Fear became my superpower
Michelle Gant

For almost as long as I can remember, I have been afraid of flying.

I don't mean metaphorically. I mean literally. Fists clenching, palms sweating, heart racing, panic rising, nausea inducing afraid.

This fear, it didn't start with my first ever flight into the great wide blue sky, a trip taken with my fellow sixth form students. I recall, with some disbelief now, that I spent take off unbothered by the machinations of the plane, instead poring over my Spanish textbook in preparation for my language exchange to Valencia. It was indeed a 'buen vuelo.'

But that was the last and perhaps only time I have taken to the sky without the trepidation which has accompanied me on pretty much every airborne journey for the last thirty years. Never mind a swimsuit and a pair of sunnies, my carry on has consisted of a little ball of terror that more than once has made me wonder if I should just sack off any ambitions to travel altogether.

At its worst, in my twenties and thirties, the little fear gremlin would take up residence the minute I put down the deposit for a week away in the sun. The excitement I would feel at the prospect of cocktails and dancing and lounging and dining al fresco would be dampened down swiftly at the prospect of the means of travel required to get there. And as much as I would try and push away all thoughts of flying until the moment of departure arrived, the worry would be constantly there, a feeling that 'something wasn't quite right.' A feeling that was only amplified when a plane would go overheard: *"That'll be me soon....."* Gulp.

If the run up to the flight was bad, then the experience once I'd pushed my (always unwieldy) case through the airport doors was awful. Every step in the procedure – check-in, security, queuing, boarding – taking me ever closer to that moment when the nose of the plane would lift off the ground and take me into the sky. As I would take my designated seat, the sound of my racing, pounding heartbeat would ring in my ears whilst my sweaty, greasy little mitts would struggle to do up the seatbelt. And you can bet that my eyes were glued to the cabin crew – who I viewed with utter awe and admiration. I mean, who would choose to do *this* for a living? – as they gave their safety demonstration. And to be honest, I would keep them in my eyeline constantly after that. I mean, if the cabin crew are still smiling then everything must be ok. Right?

More often than not, take off would bring me to tears. (And I would like to publicly apologise to my friends and family who over the years have had to endure my talons digging into them as I held onto their outstretched hands for dear life). With the panic abating somewhat, once I could see the aircraft was restored to the horizontal position, I would find myself instead throwing out sporadic questions and concerns, such as: *"What's that noise?"* or *"What's that smell?"* or *"Is it just me or does it look like that wing is falling off?"*

The arrival on terra firma was always met with absolute relief (tempered of course if the landing was just the first leg of a round trip). I'd done it. Again.

Of course, over the years, I tried to tackle my fear. I read books on overcoming the fear of flying. I tried listening to recordings that aimed to tackle my terror. I tried meditation. I did deep breathing. I wrote positive affirmations on my hands. But the method I employed most frequently to deal with my angst was a glass or two of wine pre-flight and a glass on the plane for good measure as well. (Full disclosure: I once pre ordered a bottle of champagne on a flight for my other half and I just because I knew that I would get served first and thus could have some fizz to take the edge off quicker than if I'd had to wait for the trolley service).

Unsurprisingly, my tactics never really bore fruit. For long at least. And my fear, it just became part of my identity. I wore it like a badge. If someone talked about going on holiday I would declare my aerophobia whether I was asked about it or not. *"My name is Michelle and I am terrified of flying."* It was just who I was.

Then something happened.

In 2015, the best, most magical, most incredible event occurred when I became a mum to my daughter. My beautiful girl. I wanted to be everything that I could be for her. And after our first family holiday to Sardinia, undoubtedly my favourite place to visit, I came upon a realisation.

They say you should give your children roots and wings, and I wanted to do that for my daughter. I didn't want to pass on the fear that I had had most of my life, of flying. I didn't want her to be limited like me; after all, my anxiety has meant that trips for me have never been to destinations outside Europe. I wanted her to be free, to feel untethered from worry, to not let fear hold her back.

And besides, with my beautiful daughter's arrival, I had noticed that my usual unpleasant anxiety was now coupled with something else. Guilt. Mother's guilt comes in many unwelcome forms and a new one for me was feeling guilty that I was taking my daughter away on flights. *What kind of mother was I?*

So I decided, it was high time to make a change. After all, I was sick and tired of being scared. It was....exhausting.

I decided to try hypnotherapy and thanks to some amazing therapists, my fear – wonderfully - diminished. Meaning that the time between booking and departure was no longer marked by worry, just gleeful anticipation. I didn't need to knock back a couple of stiff drinks before making my way to the departure lounge. I could walk down the tunnel to the plane without feeling like my legs were going to give way. I could browse the in-flight magazine quite calmly whilst waiting for the cabin doors to close ready for departure. How wonderful, after all those years of fraught flying.

But.

But unfortunately nothing could quite remove the discomfort that I feel on take-off. I am, after all, a woman who hasn't been on a theme park ride since I was 21, who will spend the whole day holding everyone else's coats and bags, closing my eyes whilst my loved ones partake of some thrill seeking. So no, take off feels uncomfortable to me. Which is putting it mildly.

I am also a woman who should never play poker. And so it came to pass, that a couple of years ago, I found my tears and (muffled, I thought though evidently not) squeals as the plane carried out its ascent attracting the attention of another passenger. Who thoughtfully beckoned over a member of the cabin crew who kindly sat in the aisle beside me to reassure me.

By the time we were cruising and my calm had been restored, I was in pieces. I was absolutely mortified. Here I was, trying to be a strong role model to my daughter, and I couldn't even contend with take off without embarrassing myself. I felt utterly ashamed. I felt like a total failure. Why couldn't I do what people do every day without making such a fuss? *Maybe next year we'll just stay at home.*

And yet, that might have been how I was feeling but it wasn't what my husband and daughter saw. *"Well done, you did so well. We're so proud of you." "You did it. Even though you hate it. You did it."*

Finally, the scales fell from my eyes and I realised.

Since I was 18, I have felt that my fear of flying is a weakness. A chink in my armour. Something that is negative about me. Something that is shameful. Pathetic, really.

But guess what? It's a sign of my strength. It is the catalyst for my superpower.

Because: Look. At. Me.

For three decades, I have not let that fear keep me down. I have soared in the sky almost every year to feel the sun on my face, the joy in my heart, the smile on my cheeks. I have visited new places, experienced different cultures (mostly Italian, to be fair. La dolce vita is certainly for me). I've spent time doing nothing with the people who mean the world to me. I have swum in the sea at sunrise and wondered if I would ever feel so uplifted. I have watched a red moon fill the sky and felt as if I was on another planet. I have watched a star shoot off into the distance, far above my head as if propelled by magic.

And I have done this in spite of my anxiety. I have shown myself – and my daughter – that fears aren't there to stop you. They are there to be met head on, and if maybe not quite knocked over, certainly subdued. I am the physical embodiment of feeling the fear and doing it anyway.

All the time I was worrying that I was instilling in my daughter my fear I was instead showing her that you should never let it get in the way of whatever it is what you want to do.

So what about if we all stopped thinking about the bits of us that we think of as flaws as weaknesses? What about if we saw them for what they are. Superpowers. Signs of our strength. The parts of us that show us just what we are capable of.

Maybe a bit of me will always be scared of flying. But I am absolutely not scared of living. And I will continue to soar in my own way, and I hope, I will always show my daughter that she can do the same too.

A thing learnt along the way

Take another look

'When you change the way you look at things, the things you look at change.'

Is there ever a more Monday-ish Monday than the one that comes after a holiday? However positive our mindset, however optimistic we are by nature, however refreshed we might feel, it can be a toughie to find any Monday motivation when you are going 'back to reality' after a break from the usual routine.

And so, on one such Monday, as my daughter and I got ready for the return to our usual routine of school, work, chores, and tasks, I wondered, could we think again? Think about the things that we were looking forward to that day. Seeing friends. Playing in the playground. Nice food at lunch time.

Thinking again allows for a shift in mood and focus. It allows us to see things differently, and often the view when we think again is a better one.

Embracing my uniqueness
Gemma Brown

I am always reflective around my birthday and, as I gear up to be 42 in a few days' time, I am struck by how much I still have to remind myself today of the things I wish I had known back then.

When I was younger, I wish that someone had told me that trying so hard to fit in would ultimately mean losing myself and that it would take a lifetime to unlearn all of those unhelpful patterns, followed by a lot of inner work to rediscover who I was.

At school, I so desperately wanted to be liked. I wanted to be part of all of the various groups - I wanted to be in the cool club, approachable yet fun to be around, fancied by the boys and friends with all the girls. It never struck me that being myself would be enough. So, I became very good at moulding myself into whatever I thought others wanted me to be. If they liked a particular style of music, I'd start listening to it. If they preferred certain hobbies, I'd go along with that too. I was constantly observing, adjusting, and second-guessing myself - not wanting to stand out.

When I started work, this pattern of 'fitting in' came along with me.

The result? I didn't know my own mind. I was so busy trying to match the energy, the opinions, and the personalities of others that I lost track of my own likes and dislikes. The fear of being left out or seen as 'less than' drove me to people-please to the point of exhaustion. I didn't see it for what it was at the time or how much energy it took to cover up who I really was. It was draining and unsustainable.

What I didn't understand back then was that living a life for others, wasn't really living at all. It was acting a part. And it is impossible to maintain that way of behaving if you want to live a true and fulfilling life. The irony is that bending yourself out of shape to please others only ensures that they know a version of you that doesn't really exist. So in fact, they don't really know you at all. I now know that the most important person to please is yourself.

Re-learning who you are is a journey and a daily practice, but one that is so worthwhile. The relationships you make when you bring your true self into the world, are the ones you will build a deep connection with - they will light you up rather than drain your energy.

I also wish I had understood that it is OK to take up space. I spent so much of my life shrinking myself - my thoughts, feelings and presence. I thought being agreeable, quiet and 'good' would make me more likable, but all it did was make me feel invisible -

especially when it came to stepping into the world of work. There's no reward for constantly suppressing your needs in order to make others feel comfortable. Self-compassion is knowing that you matter. You have a right to exist fully, to express yourself, and to take up as much space as you need.

I know now that the most important relationship I'll ever have is the one I have with myself and that's the one we often neglect - putting ourselves at the bottom of the priority list. When you learn to trust yourself, you stop seeking validation from others. And when you stop seeking validation, you're free to live authentically.

My final thought... it is essential that each and every one of us embraces our unique experience, individualism, views, and approach. The world doesn't need another carbon copy of what's popular, socially acceptable or 'trendy'. It needs women who are brave enough to be themselves, even when it's uncomfortable. Because when you embrace who you truly are, you not only find your own joy and fulfilment, but you also inspire others to do the same.

A thing learnt along the way

We rise by lifting others

"Compliment people. Magnify their strengths, not their weaknesses."
Joyce Meyer

Recently I came across an article online that was focused on the perceived fashion fails of famous women.

How quick our world can be to judge, to detract, to sneer, to critique others.

And indeed, this criticism and judgement may not always come from external sources. More often than not it can emanate from within.

Instead, we need to be encouragers. Supporters. We need to cheer for each other. Celebrate each other's successes. We need to have each other's backs.

I am so grateful to the women who have helped me, who have urged me on. I hold words of encouragement within me still, to revisit when I need to.

The world needs more of this. And, how awesome does it feel to be a cheerleader in this world.

After all, as the saying goes: 'we rise by lifting others.'

Lessons in friendship
Sauy Li

Looking at the picture of our smiling faces as we celebrate our friend's milestone birthday it is easy to forget how we came to be such good friends. For me the faces staring back at me are my oldest friends, we have known each other longer than we haven't and it is an achievement that was neither planned nor expected. In fact when I tell the story of my days at university it is often about the people I met and not the degree I received. It is of the laughter and moments shared between us so it is hard to believe we met because I had failed to make the grades to go to my chosen university. In fact most of us had which is now an ongoing joke!

I was eighteen and thought I knew where I was going to be spending the next three years of my life and what I would be studying but when I received my results, all of that came crashing down. Suddenly nothing was certain and there were so many decisions to be made and I had no idea if any of them would be the right ones for me. All I really knew then was that I wanted to start a new life, further my education, and hopefully realise in the process what I wanted for a career.

Which brought me to the university I didn't choose – but I'm so glad my path took me there.

In retrospect it was a terrifying time starting that chapter in my life. I was miles away from home and didn't know anyone. I was also incredibly shy and self-conscious so meeting new people filled me with dread. There was so much to learn not just in the lectures themselves but also lessons in life. It was difficult and challenging, frightening and full of uncertainty. It was also a time of possibility - of adventure and fun, late nights, happiness, tears, shenanigans – good and bad, growing up, reckless behaviour, learning to play the spoons and failing! I now know if I had let my fears and insecurities stop me from going I probably wouldn't be marking 30 years of friendship as we did last year. If I had chosen not to leave my comfort zone I wouldn't have lived this rich memorable experience with these incredible women who in one way or another have shaped the life I know. Uncertainty certainly exceeded my expectation, and I am grateful for it.

A thing learnt along the way

There is magic in the ordinary

"The art of being happy lies in the power of extracting happiness from common things."
Henry Ward Beecher

Many years ago, when my daughter was younger, she asked me if we could go to the park after school, a request I easily said 'yes' to. After all, it was on the way home.

Her response was utterly fulsome, and I glowed in her joy and gratitude for something so ordinary.

Because there is magic in the everyday. We just have to open our eyes and take a closer look.

A hug from a friend. A message from my sister. An ice-cream found at the back of the freezer (and no, I don't feel bad about keeping that discovery a secret. Finders, keepers after all). A driver letting me out at a junction. A smile. Enough milk left for a cup of tea.

Sometimes, and especially on days which might feel less rosy, I will set a challenge of looking for good stuff until I run out of things. But I always give up before the end. Because there is no end.

And sometimes, like an unplanned trip to the park,
the smallest things can yield the greatest joy.

Living by my values
Sarah Gill

In January 2023, I handed my notice in and walked away from a very well-paid job with nothing lined up to go to. Some might say it was reckless, given I was the highest earner in my household, had dependant parents, a child at university, another living in London, a large mortgage and debts. So why did I take such a leap?

At 46 years of age, having had a career that spanned over 25 years, my decision was met with a range of responses: *"What about your pension"; "You're so brave"; "You're being reactive"; "I wish I could do what you are doing!"; "Wow, good luck"*, and of course those unspoken looks that said, *"You are bonkers!"* , *"What are you doing"*, or *"Who do you think you are?".*

I began my career with such ambition to make a difference. I did not want to be that person sat in a corner complaining about the system and what was wrong, I wanted to be the person that could influence what was done about the problem. Along the way I also discovered a love for helping others grow and achieve their potential.

I had this image of my life, achievements, and career to be a very linear journey, a long ladder that required me to climb up and up until I hit the ceiling of my own potential. However what I hadn't considered was that opportunities to move up were not the only factors in building a fulfilling career.

Sixteen months before I left my job, I took on another promotion after navigating the challenges of leading through the Covid-19 pandemic. I was hopeful this would be a fresh start, but it turned out to be one of the most demanding yet rewarding roles of my career. So why did I leave? It wasn't because I shy away from challenges, in fact I generally thrive on tackling complex, knotty problems. I once had a personality profile analysis that revealed I relish high-stress situations and tend to gravitate toward solving tough issues, even when it can be self-destructive (a revelation that left me slightly unnerved at the time!) But even with that determination, I couldn't ignore how misaligned my work had become with what truly energised me.

What ultimately led me to the decision to walk away was gaining a deeper understanding of myself in the context of my situation, something that gave me the confidence to take a step that to many might seem unthinkable. This breakthrough was made possible through working with a coach. Fiona Setch, another remarkable women who is a motivational coach, enabled me to not only re-establish what was really important to me, but helped me re-discover what really made me tick, and what it was that gets the 'best' out of me and sparks joy and energy.

For the first time, I was able to articulate my core beliefs and values with clarity. I really understood for the first time the values that are intrinsic to who I am: creativity, variety, achievement, and growth. Alongside this, I came to understand my personal 'superpowers,' those qualities that I uniquely excel at: focus, high positive energy, and an innate ability to develop others.

Armed with this understanding, I evaluated my current role. On paper, everything seemed perfectly aligned and technically, it should have been an ideal match. But I faced a stark realisation that my values and superpowers were completely misaligned with the day-to-day realities of my work. The complex system I was operating within, no matter how well-intentioned, simply didn't allow me to bring these qualities to the fore. Instead, I found myself stuck in a cycle of tasks and responsibilities that drained my energy, sapped my motivation, and extinguished my passion. The things that should have fuelled me - creativity, growth, achievement, and variety - were overshadowed by activities that left me feeling unfulfilled and increasingly burnt out.

No wonder I felt a shadow of my former self. Here was me thinking I was meeting my long-term goal of being in a position of influence, but I was naively going about my work trying to 'fit a square peg into a round hole' as the saying goes. I was lacking confidence, questioning my abilities, and wondering how I'd arrived at this point. But the clarity I gained from understanding my values and superpowers helped me see that the problem wasn't me, or even my employer. It was a fundamental mismatch between who I am at my core and the role I was trying to perform at that point in time. Once I recognised this fact, it really was like someone had switched the light on in my head and life. I started to value my own worth again and the endless possibilities were before me with a renewed sense of hope and purpose. I started to see what was negotiable and non-negotiable in my life. Or what I was and wasn't prepared to put up with.

Don't get me wrong, I did and still do have occasional anxiety and the internal narrative of *'What are you doing?'*, but once I understood the key factors that make the difference for my performance, outputs, job satisfaction and general happiness, I could view the world differently. It is a bit like comparing your cheap unbranded fuel and your expensive top of the range fuel – it makes a difference! You can't fill your own tank with activities and commitments that don't match your energy or play to your strengths and expect top notch performance and outputs. You will still run okay but you may never thrive. If your work is not peppered with the things you love to do or are good at and enjoy to the very core of yourself then you are, at the very least, likely to be unmotivated, unhappy, and generally dissatisfied with your lot, and at the very worst more likely to burn out.

Two years on, I'm running my own business, helping people and teams to thrive and aspire to be more than they ever thought they could. I still have to do things that I find boring, or I have to work a bit harder to maintain my focus and interest, but at its core, my work is fuelled by doing the things that I love and I know I am good at. I assess every project and partnership through the lens of my values. If something doesn't align, I've learned to say no, even when it's tempting because it is work. To accept would not be fair to myself or the other people/project.

This mindset shift has also changed how I view success. Gone is the idealisation of a long corporate ladder that is linear and predictable. Its replaced with variety, unpredictability, and to coin a phrase from Amazing If somewhat 'Squiggly', and I love it!

One of the most transformative steps in my journey was working with a coach. If you're feeling stuck, personally or professionally, I can't recommend coaching highly enough. It provides the space to untangle thoughts, consider new possibilities, and see beyond your current perspective. A good coach won't tell you what to do but will ask the questions that lead you to your own answers.

I'll leave you with these final thoughts. I've learned some big lessons along the way, and I want to share them with you. Nothing I'm sure you haven't heard before, but a reminder that can sometimes be timely:

- It's okay to be scared and do it anyway. Fear can be a great teacher and facing it head-on often leads to the most exhilarating experiences.
- Life doesn't always go as planned and that's okay. Sometimes the best things come from the unexpected.
- Careers don't have to be linear to be successful. In fact, the most rewarding paths are often the least predictable.
- Long-term planning can be limiting. While it's good to have goals, flexibility and adaptability can open doors you never knew existed.
- Understanding your values early on is a game changer. They become your compass, guiding every decision you make.

If I'd really understood these things years ago, would I have done anything differently? Perhaps. But what I do know is this: when you understand and honour your own personal values, you don't just survive, you give yourself the opportunity to thrive.

So, if you find yourself stuck, unfulfilled, or questioning your next move, I encourage you to pause and reflect, either on your own or with an external coach. Ask yourself the following:

- What drives you?
- What energises you?
- What are your superpowers?
- What is really important to you and why?

These aren't just philosophical questions; they're practical tools for building a life and career that feel authentic and rewarding.

Take it from me: it's never too late to reassess, realign, and reimagine.

A thing learnt along the way

'In this moment, all is well'

I am a frequent time traveller.

And I imagine you are too.

There I am, doing something as innocuous as brushing my teeth or cooking the dinner and I find myself journeying back in time to previous events and happenings, making sure to pick them apart and wonder if maybe I could have done something differently. More often though, I will travel into the future and one of my fervent imagining, my path veering off track into worst case scenarios which are so vivid I can find myself quite discombobulated by the experience.

And yet, the past doesn't exist, and nor does the future. The only moment we have is now.

So when I find myself oscillating back and forth between the past and the future, I remind myself that 'in this moment, all is well', and bring myself back right now to the time that I stand in.

Another tool that I have found useful when I'm on my travels is the 5, 4, 3, 2, 1 grounding technique, which involves noticing:

- *5 things you can see*
- *4 things you can feel*
- *3 things you can hear*
- *2 things you can smell*
- *1 thing you can taste*

And in the noticing, you can ground yourself back right in the here and now. Which, after all, is the only time that exists.

Accepting grief
Marie Connell

As I get older - and hopefully a little wiser - I am surprised that life still has the habit of chucking me the odd curve ball. In March 2023 a message from my brother was such a ball. My mum had been diagnosed with stage four lung cancer - she was only in her early 70s - and had been given months to live.

My relationship with my mum had been difficult, to say the least, for many years, and we had in fact not spoken to each other for around 14 years prior to her diagnosis. Over the years we simply made each other very unhappy so we cut contact on numerous occasions. Between 2002 and 2007 we had no contact - until she needed an emergency heart operation, and prior to that she cut contact with me between 1989 and 1992 when I went to live abroad. So to get the news from my brother in 2023 led to a real mix of emotions - shock, confusion, guilt - and an extreme sadness. Sadness that she was unwell, obviously suffering, and sad about the impact of the diagnosis on the rest of my family.

However, I knew I wanted to reconnect with my mum during the last few months of her life and therefore went to visit her shortly after her diagnosis. She was obviously older and much frailer than when I had last seen her - she seemed happy to see me and we talked - just general chit chat, nothing too deep and meaningful - but for me, it was the right thing to do.

She lived less than a year - she passed away in January 2024 - and I had visited her regularly over that ten month period. I did see her just a few hours before she died; in fact all her family visited her during her last few hours, which I think she would have wanted.

One of the things I worried constantly about during Mum's illness and the period following her death, was whether, as a daughter, I was grieving properly - was I feeling sad enough? I worried that people might think I was callous or cold hearted - that I was cruel or uncaring. I lay awake at night feeling guilty that my grief was not all consuming. It took me a while but I began to realise that my grief was exactly that - MINE. It was mine to own. It was mine to feel and mine to make sense of. I started to understand that I had actually grieved for my mum years before she died - I grieved for that loving mother/daughter relationship that we never really had - I had 'lost' my mum years before, and had spent the time silently and privately grieving that loss.

For someone who has a good, healthy, and loving relationship with their parents it must be difficult to understand why we could not patch things up - or why we spent so many years out of contact. She was not the mother I needed - and I believe that I was not the daughter she wanted. It's as simple as that. I have spent years trying to come up with a different answer - an answer that will make sense to people - but there isn't one.

I have a photo wall in my home, pictures of those whom I love and care for. For years I never wanted to include a photo of my mum. But now I do have a couple of photos included in which she features, when she was healthy, happy and laughing. One is even of us out on a walk with the rest of my family and she is smiling and laughing as it was a day she got us all lost! This is how I want to remember her. This is how I want to remember our relationship. We did have some happy times together.

I wish I had known that I would come to terms with my grief, that I would accept it as mine, that I would deal with it in my own, private way and that I would come out the other end feeling a little battered and bruised - but still wanting to love my life and those people still in it. Losing a loved one is one of life's certainties - we will all grieve for someone - perhaps on numerous occasions over the years until someone grieves for us - but our own feelings of grief will be as different as we are. And that's OK.

The older I get the less I know
Claire Staddon

At thirteen I could have run the world. Sorted out all the problems that countries had with each other – probably sorted world hunger if only everyone would listen to me.

I believed that everyone had the same family experience as me, that they had the same expectations and the same horizons as me. That we were all pulling in relatively the same direction. I was naive and full of assumptions.

Don't get me wrong, I wasn't living in a fairy tale type existence of family bliss but the fundamental building blocks of things being fair – that if you work hard you get what you deserve, and if you are nice to people they will be nice to you - were family philosophies.

Over time – I would like to say gently, but let's be honest, if you go out on the adventure of life, once in a while you have to expect a few bruises - I have both broadened my experience and understanding of the complexities of life. Those philosophies are great ideals but the practical world throws a lot of shade on them.

Life is not fair – that's the truth. And something we have to accept.

Working hard does not reflect on whether you are paid properly or if you get any job satisfaction from the work.

However nice you are not everyone will be nice back – because not everyone is going to like you and you're not going to like everyone.

This has not meant that I am now a cynic and someone who is despairing; quite the contrary.

I am constantly surprised and overwhelmed with the huge capacity for compassion and joy, in my fellow human beings but it's not always where you expect to find it. The world and the human beings within it are complicated and fascinating.

Yes, I have lost that self-assurance of youth but I have gained so much more. As I head into my sixties, I am still curious and adventurous. I am still not ready for the comfortable slippers approach to life but that's me – it may not be you. I have spent the first fifty years of my life getting rid of my pre-conceptions on what good looks like and what happy feels like and that everyone else should agree with me.

My focus for the next fifty years of my life – or whatever I am gifted with (as life is a gift) is to practice routes to bring me joy. Not in an indulgent, selfish 'screw you' way, but also not asking for permission to be happy in the way I need to be. Spend time and energy on what brings you joy and recognise that those things should and can change over time. Happiness may start as owning the top-of-the-range stuff, job title, or hot holidays but be prepared to find joy in the detail, in the laughter with friends, with the success of others.

Knowing less has made me more curious and open to finding out. Anything. I am constantly fascinated by ideas, technology, and techniques that other people take for granted – as if they have always been absolute – or is that living with teenagers? It's hard learning that you don't know or have never seen something from a different perspective. It can be deeply uncomfortable - and now we are back to my Comfortable Slipper scenario again. For me finding joy is not sticking to what I know and lowering my horizons, it's lifting my eyes to what's on the other side of the hill and pushing myself to climb it. This doesn't always change my position but it always expands my understanding.

So just keep on going, keep on learning, and getting it wrong – because that's where the real lessons are. And above all else keep laughing.

A thing learnt along the way

We don't have to have all the answers

Have you ever been sitting in a meeting and been asked a question and you haven't had a clue how to respond?

Have you ever felt your anxiety and stress levels rise as you've fumbled around in your brain for the information you need?

Have you ever felt the embarrassment wash over you, feeling as if somehow you've failed?

Yep. Me too.

But the thing that I have come to learn over the years is that I don't have to have all the answers.

It's ok for me to say: "I don't know."

It's ok for me to say: "I'll come back to you on that."

It's ok for me to say: "Let me think about it."

Without embarrassment or awkwardness or sweat gathering on my brow.

It's ok to not have all the answers.

I mean, after all, we're human beings, not Wikipedia.

How will you know, if you don't try?
Sharon Clifton

Fear and anxiety are peculiar things. We think they protect us from danger, from making fools of ourselves, from messing up or making mistakes, but do they really end up making our lives better?

For years I was paralysed by a fear of ridicule, terrified I would do, say or get something so wrong I'd be a laughing stock.

Those two 'guardian angels' sat on my shoulders, whispering in my ear all the things that might happen, that could go wrong should I dare to step outside the boundaries I had set for myself. They would describe in detail how it would look, what people would say, making it difficult for me to do anything except follow the norm, stay 'within the lines', be a good girl. I was afraid to do anything out of the ordinary. They kept me safe, kept me on an easy path, held me back from the edge so I wouldn't fall.

I existed, but I never really felt alive. I was too fearful of everything. Then came a turning point, a real 'sliding doors' moment. On the occasion of my second divorce, a friend bought me a singing lesson to try to cheer me up. She knew I loved singing when I was alone, in the car, in the shower, even with her, secretly, on her daughter's karaoke machine. Her daughter was having singing lessons, so she figured it was the perfect gift for me.

Those twin detractors had always prevented me from singing in public after a bad experience trying out for the school choir when I was 11. Now they went into overdrive, trying to talk me out of going for this lesson. Eventually, about three months later, I found the strength to book that first lesson. Such was my terror at the thought of singing in front of someone, on arriving, I was gripped with fear, shaking from head to toe. The tutor put me at ease and gently encouraged me and after about ten minutes the tutor finally got a note out of me. The first time in over 30 years that I had sung, out loud, in front of a total stranger.

And this was the moment I realised that fear and anxiety had been imposters in my life. Here I was, trying something. No one laughed, nothing bad happened, windows didn't shatter. Not only had I survived the experience, but I found it emotionally cathartic and therapeutic. I booked more lessons, and my confidence grew and grew. Lots of tears were shed as the emotions that had built up inside were released.

Taking that relatively safe step and proving to myself that fear and anxiety don't always work in your favour, enabled me to start pushing at all my self-imposed boundaries. I went on to do a sky dive for Alzheimer's Society despite my crippling fear of heights, I drove a car round a racetrack, I went on holiday alone, and I've even started my own company.

In addition, I am now performing regularly in public with The Fried Pirates, a folk and Americana Band I have been with for 10 years, and am now in two duos – Peddars Way and The Rummuns. I've even stepped into the very exposing arena of writing song lyrics with the support of my bandmate Chris Moorhouse.

My point is none of us know what skills, talents, or genius we have inside of us. Any of us could be amazing dancers, artists, flower arrangers, writers, actors, sports people, musicians, explorers, astronauts - but not if we never try because we let our inner critic rule us like I did. Life is too short to let fear hold you back. Whatever your passion, don't be afraid to try, challenge those negative voices and ask yourself: *"What is the worst thing that can happen?,"* and *"Are you ok with that?"* Take that first step. You might just discover something extraordinary about yourself.

Fill your life doing more of the things that light you up, rather than lurking in shadows and watching everyone else do it.

Don't get me wrong, it's not easy. It's a constant battle, and still the anxiety rears its head from time to time. And not everything I try is successful, but I'm learning to embrace the journey and trying not to take myself so seriously. If I laugh at myself, I feel that people are laughing with me, not at me. And whether it's true or not, it's enough for me to keep fear and anxiety at arm's length and be able to enjoy life.

Make time to talk
Steph Allen

My dad was the manager of the North London branch of a national life assurance company. Through my years living at home I watched as he dealt with queries from people at, invariably, the worst times of their life. They contacted the office to claim their loved ones' life assurance. I didn't realise it at the time, but Dad had an unwritten rule that he would talk with everyone who rang or wrote to report a death. The usual office procedures would be followed, however, my dad would visit each claimant to pay out the policy personally. This didn't appear at all odd to me! It was quite common for him to drive me to school, go to the office, pick me up, and take me home (I was clearly a lazy child, but there again, we were in a busy London suburb) and then drive to a grieving widow in the East End to offer condolences and pay the policy out.

I recall one Christmas Day in the early 1960s, we had just started our Christmas lunch. The phone rang, and as was the norm in those days, no voicemail facility meant that we would always answer it. My dad went into the hall, and for some twenty minutes was talking in a soft voice to the caller. On his return to the dining room, he apologised but explained that it was a client and her husband died on Christmas Eve. She knew how kind my dad had been in the past and knew he'd talk to her! This situation came back to me recently, when I was in a debate on LinkedIn about taking time out and wellbeing.

How easy it would have been to ignore the call, but: *"It might be important / serious / bad news / a Christmas wish from a long lost relative!"* How easy it would have been to cut the call short, by saying he would ring her back after Boxing Day. How easy it would have been not to care. But of course, in those days communication was very different.

Now of course, we have the constant ability to interact and connect, almost whether we like it or not! Let's replay the scenario with today's tech. Clients would report a death on a central website and probably receive email confirmation that their claim was being dealt with. There would be no personal contact, no metaphorical hug, no sense of caring.

It may be that my dad could have given clients his email address, but we are all encouraged not to check our work tech during holidays. Whatever the scenario now, this grieving client would not have had someone to listen to her!

Now, it's fair to say, that despite being a baby boomer, I am hugely fond of modern tech! My iPhone and iPad are, it has been said, surgically attached to me at all times and, I'm ashamed (?) to say, that whilst staying in a beautiful hotel in North

Norfolk, I almost had a meltdown because there was no Wi-Fi! There are huge benefits to modern day communication, however maybe personal contact isn't one!

The convenience of finding information quickly, or the ability to take photos (hundreds!) of your cat, children or a beautiful plate of food, or paying for goods with a tap of your phone, or sending a happy face emoji to cheer up a friend, or contributing to family WhatsApp groups, or following maps and Sat-Nav, or keeping boarding passes to hand, or controlling central heating, are all benefits of our modern tech!

The one action, conspicuous by its absence, is using our smartphones as…… telephones!

And this is my learning! My natural instinct is never to use my phone as a phone. I tell myself that if I call someone: *"I might interrupt their work"*, or *"They may be sitting down to eat"*, or *"They may not want to talk"*, or *"Do I want to talk?"* Am I making excuses to barricade myself behind tech?   Why do I, and so many others, fall back into the easy option of non-verbal telephonic interaction: text, WhatsApp, Messenger, and all text-based actions?

I don't pretend to know the answer, but I have learned over the years, that whether you're a baby boomer, generation X, millennial, generation Z, or alpha, there are times when only a voice will do! It is definitely, in my opinion, helpful to conduct most administrative connections online, rather than ring a call centre and listen to endless Muzak. However, having the opportunity to just talk with someone is a huge blessing. We, as a society, are losing a sense of compassion and empathy by not creating verbal communication opportunities, however strong the pull towards apps and internet-based activities is.

What I've learned when thinking back to my beloved dad is that however we admire and maximise the huge benefits of tech, there are times and will always be times when human interaction, a voice, and a listening ear will be an absolute necessity! I had no idea, watching the way he worked, the way he cared for all his clients and the way he showed compassion, that his values would be in jeopardy as the world absorbed technology!

It has hit me particularly hard because it's taken me many years of boasting about all the things I can do with my devices, none of which include talking with people, before I suddenly had that flashback to how my dad worked!

In a way, the seduction by technology overwhelmed me and I have forgotten the key tenets of human interaction. My dad set an example that I allowed to be overtaken in time.

I may prefer to text, use Messenger, WhatsApp, or any other method of communicating, but this world will be a poorer place without verbal communication! I wish I'd realised this when I was younger, if I'm honest, I almost begrudged the fact that he was out seeing his clients at strange times, but he was offering them exactly what they needed, another human being's compassion!

Let's continue to use our smartphones but let's make time to talk! Thank you dear Dad!

A thing learnt along the way

Listening is an act of love

"Listening is one of the loudest forms of kindness."
Unknown

*One of the kindest, most powerful things we can do
for each other is listen. Truly, attentively, supportively
listen. And the more we listen, the more people will
feel safe and empowered to talk.*

*Love, respect, kindness is shown by truly listening to
someone; it's one of the best ways we can
demonstrate to people that we care.*

*Stopping and patiently paying attention to what
someone has to say is a kindness that can be
transformative.*

And it feels good to listen.

*But it's not just about listening to others. It's about
taking the time to listen to ourselves, and truly
hearing our hopes, dreams, fears, and everything else
that runs through us.*

It is ok to be you (however that looks)
Luisa Stanney

Growing up I didn't really feel like I fitted in well. I felt I wasn't clever enough, thin enough and I wasn't one of the gang of girls at secondary school that were popular. I was always somewhere in the middle. This followed me into married life when my ex-husband and I were friends with a group of people who I didn't feel like I fitted in with.

Over time I have learned that I do not have to be friends with people to please anyone and as a consequence my circle of friends around me now are my 'ride or dies' who have seen me through all of my highs and lows. My two sons who are now 25 and 21 are also very good judges of character and tell me quite plainly 'how it is' which has helped me immensely with my resilience over the past few years when it has just been us three navigating our way through life.

I wish I could tell myself 25 years ago that I didn't have to always please everyone else, that it was ok to sometimes put yourself first for the sake of your mental health, happiness, stability, and finances.

Getting divorced from my ex-husband was extremely difficult, especially after losing my mum when I was pregnant with my second son a few years previously. I had lost my family unit that I loved and my extended family and suddenly it was just me and my two boys juggling life. But we did it. We even had fun along the way exploring different places and going on holiday with my sister and her family.

But then bang! I found myself in another relationship that lasted nine years. I lost myself in the relationship. In 2023 I ended the relationship.

The last two years have been a bumpy road. I have had to have counselling and was on antidepressants. My mind played tricks on me and I started to question whether I had done the right thing, ending a relationship, and those rose-tinted glasses kept going back on. I felt lonely, confused, and unlovable and all those earlier feelings from my younger years came back.

I think my previous relationships have taught me that I should always trust myself and my gut instincts.

I have also learnt along the way that I do not need to change for anyone - we should all feel able to just be ourselves.

I have used the last two years to try different things. I have taken my Level Two and Three in Counselling, which has helped me understand that I cannot fix everything for everyone and don't have to have all the answers. I met some great people whilst at college and have gone on to pass my Level Two in

Safeguarding. Whether I choose to use these skills in a future career remains to be seen, but it has helped in my current job where I am a mental health first aider for the company I work for which has helped me understand people better.

I have also tried things that I would never have done if I was in a relationship - joined a choir with my friend (it didn't last long - we weren't exactly Mariah and Whitney!) I help a friend with their mobile bar business (who knew I had an inner Bet Lynch!), and I've been on holiday with my eldest son, my youngest son and his girlfriend, and other things.

My eldest son has now gone to Australia for at least a year and my younger son is away at university. I am immensely proud of them both. I miss them both lots, but I am going to use the time now to find out what it is I want to do/be. If Mr Right (think Tom Hardy crossed with Ray Winstone and a bit of Danny Dyer wearing a tool belt) comes along then great, but if he doesn't, then I am going to work bloody hard at making sure I am ok with just being me. Everything I have gone through in life has made me who I am today, an extremely proud mum to two independent sons who are exploring the world. I try to be a good mum, sister, daughter, work colleague, and friend to my 'ride or dies' and I am there for them as much as they are for me - and if all else fails at least I can pull a bloody good pint in a crisis!

"Accept the things you cannot change, have the courage to change the things you can and the wisdom to know the difference," - Karl Paul Reinhold Niebuhr

A thing learnt along the way

Life is life

One sunny, summer day, I was sitting with my friend on a bench. My friend had had a shattering diagnosis a few years ago and we were updating each other on things that were happening for us.

"Life is shite," I said, a knee jerk remark to the news she was sharing with me.

"No," she replied, "Life is life," she said, calmly, serenely, sincerely.

It was a comment that struck me profoundly then, and the words have stayed with me ever since. Whenever I find myself raging against things, I remind myself 'life is life.'

Sometimes it's beautiful, glorious, uplifting, and magical, so spectacular it fills your heart fit to burst. Other times it's heart wrenching, agonising, painful, and you wonder how you will get through the days. And the rest of the time it's just there, carrying on quietly.

Life is life.

My dear friend Gemma is no longer here but her words stayed with me. And, to paraphrase what she wrote in the essay for my first book 'When The World Paused':

Life…. 'breathe it in.'

Life can change in an instant and you only get one shot - make it count!
LJ

Trigger warning: please note this essay contains themes of suicide and baby loss.

From an early age, family was so important to me. The relationship my parents had was fab. They had been together since grammar school; they supported each other, made family life fun and the love we had for each other was amazing. Whether it was watching the A-Team (showing my age now!) on a Saturday afternoon, days out in the countryside with a picnic, shopping sprees, get togethers with friends and family, or watching a movie, we were always together. I was a 'daddy's girl', he was my hero and we were very close. So, you can imagine how my world imploded when, in my early teens my dad passed away suddenly after a short illness, and our little family was torn apart.

I realised I had to grow up quickly, to support my mum if nothing else as I could see her crumbling, both emotionally and physically, before my eyes. There were no counselling services for children back then, but I considered myself very lucky to have amazing friends (some of whom I see as family), who were by my side whenever I needed them, even before mobile phones and social media were a thing!! On reflection, I'm not sure whether losing my dad spurred me on to recreate the relationship my parents had and replace the family life I had lost so abruptly, perhaps it did. However, after buying a house with my first love (from school, whom I hoped was 'the one') and facing up to the realisation that we both wanted different things from life, I forced myself to move on.

By this point, my mum and I had developed an immensely strong bond; we were a force to be reckoned with and had the most laughs and the best of times. Our bond had strengthened as we navigated her first battle with cancer together. She became my inspiration. I was in awe at her unwavering strength and determination to live (not just survive). Even when she was feeling at her lowest after chemotherapy. I remember sitting and having a conversation with her one day about children and how, at times, it was hard being an only child. At the time she was dealing with sorting out her parents' will. She said it must be much easier to deal with stuff like this when there's a sibling to lean on. I remember agreeing and reassuring her that I'd have more than one child; seemed like a good plan!

Around this time, I had a short relationship with a great guy who helped to fix my wings that were left broken after the end of my previous relationship. We had very little in common, but we laughed, talked for hours, cooked great food, and loved each other for the short time that we had together. I knew he wasn't 'the one', but he was the right person at the right time and that was all that mattered.

Unfortunately, I never saw his suicide coming and I was left reeling from the shock of, not only finding him that day, but also from losing someone who had put me at the centre of his world and made me feel worthy again. I had experienced grief before with the loss of my dad (and most of my grandparents by then), but I soon realised that losing someone to suicide is a whole different ball game. I felt like I was in a 'bubble', asking myself questions that I would never get answers to like why, could I have done anything to save him, did I do something wrong? I know now that there was absolutely nothing I could have done but back then I felt so vulnerable and just lost really.

Around the same time, a friend of mine was also grappling with grief after the loss of his fiancée. I could see he was struggling even more than I was, both physically and emotionally, and I wanted to help. We had known each other a few years, and we were happy to prop each other up through those first tough months. He was very helpful when I moved into my new house, even cleaning up! I was so grateful that someone had taken the reins whilst I was still navigating my way through my own grief and learning to live on my own. We began to spend more time together, we became quite dependent on each other. I found we had the same likes and dislikes, wanted the same family life, similar views to parenting, retirement plans, and such like. He had mentioned a couple of times that we could be more than just friends, but I had been dismissive up to that point as something didn't feel right; maybe it was too soon I thought? However, the more I looked at our unique situation and how well things seemed to be working, I couldn't ignore the fact that my ideal partner might be standing straight in front of me - my mum and friends agreed!

Things moved quickly once we'd made the decision to give the relationship a go. He moved in within a couple of months, proposed a few months later and a year after, we were married. It was a wonderful day, surrounded by our family and friends, a celebration of our love and a day I'm sure my mum believed she wouldn't live to see. She looked so beautiful as she passed my hand across to my new husband, confident that her daughter would now have the life and family that she had yearned so long for.

My mum's cancer had unfortunately returned and there was no cure this time. Again, she didn't let it stop her from doing everything she wanted to do; even when the treatment made her feel ghastly, she could still laugh at the silliest of things, that would send us both into absolute hysterics. I was not ready to say goodbye to her, but that summer the decision was taken from me and she passed away.

I'm sorry to say that my mum was not the only loss that week, as I had also gone into premature labour and lost our first baby. I felt I had failed as a mother as I had not been able to keep my baby safe, and all I wanted was to seek comfort from my own mum, who was no longer there. Again, a new sort of grief; losing a parent (of which I was familiar with), but also losing a child. I can honestly say my heart ached in places I never knew existed, and once again I was lost.

I was in desperate need of a 'grown up' to support me, so I turned to some friends of my parents, a therapist, and of course, my faithful friends, who were invaluable. After what seemed like being in an emotional daze for months, my husband and I agreed that we still wanted a family and the summer after, we welcomed a beautiful daughter. For the first time in years, I felt complete with her nestled in my arms. She was perfect.

I understood relationships change once you have children, but I was ready and excited that we were now parents. However, our daughter wasn't a great sleeper, perhaps because I was reluctant to let go of her, and I found that I was the one consumed with her care. At first, I embraced it as a shiny, new mum as it confirmed I was providing everything my baby needed. As most new mums do, I got used to surviving on very little sleep, eating cold food and being proud of myself if I managed to get out of the house fully dressed, with my baby fed and fully dressed, and without one of my boobs hanging out. I was living the dream!

However, the same could not be said for my relationship with my husband as things changed. I would always try and talk to him and I would ask what I could do.....clearly I was being a good mum, but (in my head) I obviously wasn't being a good wife, so I had to try and make things better.

I'm not going to lie to you, that first year was blooming hard. I lost count of the times I sat and cried, wondering what I was doing wrong and trying to reassure myself that I was keeping everyone happy. I made sure I did this in private (usually in the shower). Everything would be absolutely fine and then it was like something would snap and it would be back to that dark place again. I remember opening up to my close friends to see if this was normal; was this just how marriage and family life was? I knew them all so well and their looks said it all. They were all truly supportive.

So, now what was I to do?! I married for life; that was my stance, and I was determined that I could make things better. However, it became clear that my hopes of more children would not be realised. I found myself questioning my marriage, realising I wasn't going to fulfil the dream I had chatted to my mum about that day, whilst clinging to my daughter and sobbing; this was not the way I had expected family life to be.

As the years rolled on, the emotional rollercoaster continued. Don't get me wrong, we had some amazing times and made great memories, but on the flip side to that when the rollercoaster dipped, there are memories I wish I could forget. Sometimes it felt like I was going crazy, and I would doubt myself regularly. But, whilst all this was happening, I would of course maintain my smiley exterior even though inside my emotions were churning.

Luckily, therapy has taught me to compartmentalise and validate my emotions and thoughts. I separated from my husband just over a year ago, as I realised that I had lost the 'real me' and I didn't recognise who I was when I was with him. I had to heal myself, and I couldn't do that if we stayed together as it was apparent that my healing wasn't happening fast enough. I admit, I am not blameless in all this, I am guilty of sticking my head in the sand and putting on a brave face. The hardest decision I have ever had to make, but I know deep down it was the right one for me, and for my daughter.

People never imagine that they will experience these kinds of loss and trauma in their life. Therapy has taught me that even when these events occur in life, you can heal and learn from them; not overnight, but it's a journey. I am on that healing journey, and gradually the full version of me is returning. My friends maintain that I've always been me, but sometimes a watered-down version. This last year, I have had difficult conversations and dealt with challenging issues, and people have shown themselves for who they truly are. The difference now, and thanks to months of therapy, is that I believe them the first time.

I am proof that you can experience the most unimaginable loss, grief, separation, and lead a joyous, full life, loving and living with my wonderful daughter by my side. I am so very proud of her; she continues to thrive in everything she does and is growing up to be a very astute and emotionally intelligent young lady (she must have her grandmother's genes!). I know that new people will join me on this journey called life (which I intend to live to the full, by the way), and I will welcome them with open arms whilst also treading with an element of caution! As I always say to my daughter (however much it makes her cringe!), always be yourself and be true, as those that matter won't mind, and those that mind; don't matter.

A thing learnt along the way

There is always hope, there is always help

"Realise that you are not alone, that we are in this together and most importantly there is hope."
Deepika Padukone.

Whatever is going on in our lives, whoever we are, and wherever we are, we are not alone.

Friends, family, professionals, and strangers – maybe even the strangers whose words within these pages are resonating with you – there are people who we can connect with.

Whatever we are going through, and within the midst of any struggle, we always need to remember that there is someone who can lend a listening ear, a helping hand, and hope can be found.

Follow your own path and not the path of expectations
Sam James

...To say no to things. To choose not to do things. To say yes to the things that make me come alive or feel right for me. To explore the things that make my heart sing, rather than sink.

Reaching your potential or being successful doesn't have to be based on everyone else's hopes and expectations for you. You don't have to chase the social norms for what we are told we should aspire to – the job, the house, the status.

I was academically capable, which I am grateful for because it gave me options. But it also led to many of years of questioning whether I have 'fulfilled my potential'? And there are still times that I spiral down a hole with that question. That pressure hasn't come from my parents. They have only ever encouraged me to pursue the things that I wanted to. Yes, there was encouragement to consider other things that maybe I hadn't thought about, to keep my aspirations open, but there was never a strong push to follow any particular path.

The pressure I have felt has come from societal 'norms'. The well-meaning comments from people around me (teachers, other adults, family friends, peers). Teachers who wanted to inspire me and wanted me to fulfil my potential. My peers at university. Everyone seemed to be on a clearly defined career trajectory at 18 years old. I had no idea! I was there because I loved psychology and fell in love with the university on the open day. I didn't know what I was going to do at the end of those three years.

I've spent the past 15 years of my adult life supporting women to find out what it is they want to pursue, to live life on their terms; whilst always being aware that I am always trying to give myself the same gift.

But it is hard. It is hard not to get swept into things, because we think 'we should'.

I have found myself applying for jobs, or continuing with projects, because 'it's what I should be doing'. Feeling like if I am not working hard enough, or doing it right, if I am not 'busy', or not as 'frazzled' as those around me or if I don't have a 'proper' recognisable job title.

But what I know, intellectually and on a feelings level, is that the times when I am thriving, are when I am spending my time living life from a place of the things that genuinely make my heart sing. Not from a place of 'shoulds'.

Now, what those things are for me, is going to be completely different to what those things are for you. And that's OK. It's more than OK. It's what makes the world a vibrant place to be.

Imagine what it could be like if everyone felt accepted and able to live life in a way that felt good for them.

Imagine what life would be like if we celebrated JOMO (the joy of missing out), rather than tried to avoid FOMO (the fear of missing out).

Imagine how liberating it would be if we just stopped trying to fit into different shaped holes full stop; square or round ones.

Imagine if we knew we all belong, as we are, with our strengths and our individual preferences and needs. That we can live life on our terms, pursuing the things that make us feel alive. And that is being 'successful' at living. That is being truly happy.

As a parent this is something, I want for my children more than anything. Although, it is hard not to then look at it through the glasses of societal norms and expectations. I am curiously watching, how comfortable they both are about knowing the things that they don't want to do (as well as things they do). When we've chatted about whether to go to parties, or pursue opportunities at school, they have both been able to explain that they know they won't feel comfortable and enjoy certain things, and they don't want to force themselves and end up feeling not great, and potentially their friends picking up on that. They are able to be honest with friends, that *"I just can't do sleepovers like that because I need sleep,"* or *"I don't like discos, and find them really difficult."* I'm not going to lie, as a parent I struggled with this initially because I was worried they wouldn't get invited to things and be socially isolated. That isn't what's happened. They have friends who understand them. They spend time together doing things they will all enjoy together. And, when it comes to inviting their friends to do things, they also are able to say: *"I'm not sure if you'll feel comfortable doing this thing, and that's OK, we can do something else together that we can both enjoy."* I've found it interesting noticing my own internal struggle with this though; I want nothing more than for my children to know themselves and feel confident to live life in a way that means they can thrive; I also want them to 'fit in' – but remind myself, that what I actually want more than anything is for them to be themselves and belong. They will be able to find the places and people they belong with, by knowing themselves and not forcing themselves to fit.

I wish someone had taken my hand when I was younger, and invited me to get to know myself (not the career test I took!) – what matters most to me, what makes me feel energised and alive, when I feel most comfortable in myself, and what I love. Then I could have used this as a compass to help me navigate the paths I explored, with a quiet confidence about the choices that I was making. So, start asking yourself why? Why am I choosing to do this? Why do I think this is the thing to pursue? If you notice 'shoulds' in there, check-in with yourself, and gently question and explore what is behind the should. Chase the things that make you feel alive, the things that matter for you, in a way that means you can show up wholeheartedly as you. That is where true success lies.

Know your purpose, trust your instincts, and stay present
Lisa Collen

- **Consider the why.**

Whilst driving and listening to the radio, the presenters were asking each other funny and awkward questions from job interviews. Questions such as: *"If you were an animal, what animal would you be?"; "What's the one thing you won't miss from your current job?," and "What's the one question you were glad we didn't ask you?"* Having been an interviewer and been interviewed, I realised it's not necessarily the answer they are interested in, but the reasons behind that answer - the 'why' moment. That tells so much about you. So always ask yourself why.....why did I say or think that, why did I do that, why is that the way forward, why, why, why! As a child, we ask lots of why questions.....remember to consider the why as that is where the true thinking sits. And maybe avoid saying 'a sloth' if asked about the animal question (unless you have a good reason why!).

- **Trust your instincts**.

And don't overthink things. Someone has made a fortune after honing the five second rule. Acting on their first thought. My understanding of their concept is after five seconds of making a decision, we start to talk ourselves out of it. *"I'm going to do that,"* but quickly we hear ourselves saying: *"That's dangerous, it could go wrong, what's the risk?".* So hold onto that first thought. Do consider the risk, impact, reasons why, but don't lose sight of the decision you made within those first five seconds. Our instincts as human beings have enabled us to survive for this long!

- **Stay in the present.**

Eckhart Tolle is the author of The Power of Now. It refers to the concept of mindfulness and reminds us to remain present. When we think about the past or the future, it causes us to be unsettled or feel a sense of unease – another work for unease is dis-ease, or more commonly known as disease. We can't change the past, but we can learn from it. We can't guarantee the future, or anything beyond this moment. So give yourselves a moment to stop, think, and be. Someone once told me to carry an invisible bench in my pocket and remember to get it out and sit on it sometimes. By doing so, I remain in the present and can take in the pleasure of being here right now......and writing this reflection to share with you lovely people.

A thing learnt along the way

Small steps will help you travel far

I am always coming up with new dreams, things that I would love to do, ambitions that my heart aches to achieve (like this gorgeous book).

But, in creating these goals, I can feel overwhelmed by the gap between where I am and where I want to be, disheartened to the point that I often think about sacking it off as a non-starter before I've even begun.

The thing I've learnt is to take a breath. Then ask myself: "What's the very first thing I can do?" It might be as simple as to tell someone what the goal is (which is what I did with this book). That's a step forward.

An then another one. Then another. And before you know it you've travelled further than you could have ever imagined.

So keep on dreaming big. Don't let the size of your goals put you off. You don't have to take a giant leap forward; tiny actions, the little things you do will take you ever closer to where you want to be.

Plus, the more small steps you take, the more your confidence and belief in yourself to achieve your dreams will grow.

Find who you've always been
Rebecca Price

The things I wish I'd known. Where do I start?!

Thankfully there's a big difference between what I wish I'd known and what advice I'd have given myself. If I'd been given advice, I probably wouldn't have listened to it. Because I was pretty headstrong.

But where I'd start would be understanding the importance of being kind to myself and giving myself a break. No matter how hard I was on those around me (and I was), I was hardest of all on myself. Every mistake I made, every wrong step taken, I was furious at myself and would reflect endlessly on what I should have done but didn't. Change what you can, don't grieve for what you can't. Apologise if you need to, do things differently next time, put it down to experience. In fact I wish I could go back in time and give myself a big hug. I was in such need of them and yet unwittingly did everything I could to push hugs away.

When I was a girl, I wasn't the captain of the netball team. People usually didn't want me on their rounders team, because I'd probably made them lose the last time around. I wasn't good at the things it was cool to be good at. I had a navy blue Burberry raincoat rather than the purple maxi-coat I wanted. I was a bit quirky and a bit odd. I wish I'd known there would come a time when people would regard difference as a superpower – and that I'd come to realise that too. I wish I'd been sufficiently self-aware not to waste years compensating for what I wasn't and didn't and couldn't when I was a child.

I wish I'd known that some of the advice you are given is complete rubbish. *'The harder I work, the luckier I get'*. Nope. You also need luck and opportunity. Not only is it possible to be great, hard-working and not succeed, you'll also meet a whole load of people who've succeeded on their unwavering self-belief and ability to play the game, alone. Which takes us nicely onto *'fake it until you make it'*. Not a great idea. I wish I hadn't disguised my total lack of confidence with a pretence of one.

It's important to recognise good advice too. *'Smell the roses'*. Make the most of every pleasant thing that happens, every single thing that goes right. Because *'nothing ever lasts forever'* and that's worth knowing too, when things seem irretrievably awful. When good happens, wrap your arms around it and relish it. When bad happens, in time, it will pass.

There's so much more I wish I'd known. Don't ever start drinking wine. It's not a good idea to sunbathe. Soap isn't skincare. Sleep really does matter. And of course, you're not as fat as you think.

But I'd also want myself to know there was stuff I

was getting right, even if the world was telling me I was wrong. Calling out sexism, did not make me popular at times and nor did it make an immediate difference. But I was right and now our workplace is very different from the one I first entered in the '80s. I was right to make a huge fuss about smoking in the office and it's hard to believe people did so as recently at the early 'noughties'. Being headstrong meant I'd call out things that, in time, would never be tolerated.

But above all, rather than longing to have all the right answers, I wish I'd known that's missing the point. In fact, rather than telling our younger selves what we ought to have known, I wonder what advice our younger selves might give to us, as we are now? My younger self might congratulate me on and feel good about what I have achieved. Whereas my current self focuses too much on what I haven't. My younger self might tell me it's not too late to give up the wine! She might also tell me that I still don't have all the answers and that it's important to continue to be curious, questioning, challenging, a work-in-progress and chasing the next big hurrah.

Not knowing the answers, making mistakes, being ridiculous, getting it wrong – and getting it right – are all part of life. And they're not just the sole preserve of the young. In fact if there's one thing, above all, I'd like my younger self to know, it's this. Find the person you were, before all the nonsense in life kicked in. Maybe it was when you were three or five or seven. Find them and embrace them, because underneath it all, that's who you are today. And she's just fine.

What the menopause has taught me
Vicki Haverson

If there's one thing I've learned from my journey through menopause, it's that understanding and finding the right support can be challenging. Menopause isn't just the end of one phase of life; it's a transformation that affects every part of who you are—from your physical health to your sense of self. If I'd had some of this insight years ago, it could have spared me a lot of frustration and heartache. For anyone else embarking on this path, here are the key things I wish I'd known, and what I have learnt on my personal journey through the menopause.

Early signs: recognising perimenopause
The earliest signs of perimenopause started for me in my late thirties, and they caught me off guard. I'd often heard menopause was something that happened in your fifties, but for me, the symptoms began much earlier. I started experiencing headaches, overwhelming fatigue, anxiety, and mood changes that I couldn't explain. My periods became heavy and unpredictable, sometimes so intense and painful I feared leaving the house. Each of these issues felt isolated, and I didn't realise at first they might be connected. Knowing now how early hormonal changes can start would have saved me years of worry and confusion.

I wish I'd known back then that symptoms like mood swings, anxiety, fatigue, and even joint pain can be signs of perimenopause. It's not always the sudden, textbook 'hot flushes' that signal hormonal changes. Perimenopause can begin a decade or more before menopause itself, and recognising these early signs can make a world of difference in getting the right support.

Trust your instincts: advocating for your health
Early on one of the biggest obstacles I encountered was finding medical support that recognised my symptoms as hormone-related. I saw several doctors and specialists, but the advice I received was often dismissive or focused on managing individual symptoms without addressing the root cause. At the time I was living overseas and it wasn't until I saw a hormone specialist that I felt someone truly understood what I was going through.

My experience taught me to trust my instincts and advocate for myself, even when my concerns were dismissed. Keeping a symptom diary was immensely helpful; it allowed me to clearly communicate my experiences and track patterns over time. This became crucial when discussing options with healthcare providers, especially those who might not specialise in menopause. For anyone feeling lost in the medical system, don't be afraid to seek second opinions and bring in notes, questions, and research to your appointments.

Hormone therapy isn't one-size-fits-all
While I recognise that private healthcare isn't affordable or accessible for everyone, I found it crucial to seek out specialists who understood the nuances of HRT and menopause. I found that resources like Dr Louise Newson's Menopause Doctor website and podcast, as well as Davina McCall's book and documentary on menopause, provide a wealth of accessible, evidence-based advice. Davina's work helped me understand the breadth of experiences women go through, and her honest discussions on HRT and symptom management are incredibly validating.

Quitting alcohol: one of the best decisions I made
While hormonal support played a major role, for me, lifestyle changes also helped me manage symptoms. I'd been using alcohol as a way to cope with my mood swings and anxiety, but I came to realise that it was actually exacerbating my symptoms. Deciding to quit drinking wasn't easy, but looking back, it's one of the best decisions I've made for my health. Seven years on, I've never felt better for it, and it allowed me to gain clarity and control over my symptoms and emotions.

Exercise also became an essential part of my routine. When I discovered CrossFit, I found it empowered me both physically and mentally. Strength training not only improved my energy levels but also gave me a sense of resilience that spilled over into other areas of life. Maintaining a nutrient-rich diet with plenty of vegetables, lean proteins, and healthy fats also helped, especially in balancing my mood and energy.

The impact on teeth and eyes: unwelcome surprises
One of the most distressing and surprising aspects of my menopause journey were the issues with my teeth and eyes. My teeth became increasingly problematic, with infections that wouldn't heal, leading to the loss of two teeth. It was incredibly upsetting, and it wasn't until later that I learned this can be a common issue for women going through menopause, linked to dropping estrogen levels which can impact oral health. Menopausal women can experience thinning enamel, gum disease, and even tooth loss due to hormonal changes.

Around the same time, I started experiencing issues with my eyes—they were constantly tearing up, and at times, I struggled to keep them open. An optometrist diagnosed me with severe dry eyes, and it turned out that hormonal changes can also affect eye moisture, leading to this uncomfortable condition. These health issues were another reminder that menopause affects many parts of your body, and how important it can be to pay attention to symptoms that may seem unrelated to hormones.

Sleep disruptions: waking up early
Another frustrating aspect of perimenopause for me

was sleep disruption, particularly waking up at 4 a.m. It was a pattern that left me feeling drained and frustrated. This is actually quite common during perimenopause and is linked to hormonal fluctuations—especially a drop in estrogen just before your period. I learnt that estrogen helps regulate your sleep cycle, and when its levels drop, it can lead to difficulty staying asleep. In addition, the decrease in progesterone, which has a calming effect, can make it harder to stay asleep through the night. Anxiety and stress, common during this time, can also contribute to restless nights.

I also found that night sweats were an issue I struggled with, adding to my early wake-ups. If you're struggling with sleep disruptions, it's important to know that you're not alone, and I discovered there are strategies like relaxation techniques, sleep hygiene practices, and even supplements that can help.

My relationship with my husband: a new kind of challenge

Menopause isn't just about managing symptoms within your own body - it can have a significant impact on your relationships too. I've been with my husband for over 20 years, but during the menopause, I found myself feeling like I couldn't stand him at times. My moods were all over the place, and the emotional rollercoaster of menopause made it hard to connect with him in the way I had before.

It was a tough phase, and we struggled to communicate at times. My experience was that once I started hormone replacement therapy (HRT), the difference was like night and day. The irritability that I couldn't seem to control softened, and I could finally see the man I had loved for over two decades again. Relationships can be tricky to navigate during this time, and menopause can often feel like an emotional upheaval that's hard to explain. But I think one of the most important lessons I've learned is to talk openly with my partner. Understanding that these changes are temporary (with the right support) has brought us closer and strengthened our relationship.

Navigating the medical system: persistence pays off
After multiple consultations over the last few years, I connected with a head pharmacist at my local practice, who reviewed my case history and agreed to support the hormonal treatments recommended by a private specialist. This experience taught me that while there are often barriers in the medical system, persistence does pay off. Building a supportive network of healthcare providers can make all the difference.

The importance of support: talking to friends
One of the greatest sources of strength I found

during this time was talking to friends. Menopause can be isolating, but having a group of women to confide in, share experiences, and swap advice with made a huge difference. Whether it's about symptoms, treatment options, or just the emotional rollercoaster of it all, having people to speak to who really understand makes a world of difference.

Connecting with others who are experiencing similar things can help you feel seen and heard. In addition to professional advice, it was the informal support from friends who shared their own journeys that helped me navigate my own. It's something I can't overstate enough—don't bottle it all up. Talking about it makes it easier to bear.

Resources I found helpful
Navigating menopause can feel like uncharted territory, but several resources became lifelines got me along the way. I found Davina McCall's book and documentary on menopause incredibly validating, helping me understand that I wasn't alone in my symptoms or frustrations. I also found Dr Louise Newson's Menopause Doctor website and podcast invaluable, offering practical advice and evidence-based guidance that helped me make informed decisions about my care. Kelly Casperson's book, *You Are Not Broken*, also became a fantastic resource for understanding how common it is to feel 'off track' during menopause and gave me strategies for managing the emotional aspects of the process.

For anyone beginning this journey, I recommend exploring books, podcasts, and articles on menopause, especially those created by menopause specialists. The knowledge you gain can be empowering and help you make the best decisions for your health.

Embracing menopause as a time of transformation
Menopause is often seen as an ending, but it can also be a time of significant personal growth. My journey taught me that menopause isn't something to just 'get through' but an opportunity to understand myself and my needs in a deeper way. Today, I feel more resilient, self-aware, and willing to advocate for what I need—qualities I didn't always have before.

To anyone beginning this journey, know that you're not alone. The path may be full of unexpected twists, but with the right resources, support, and persistence, you can find a way to feel like yourself again. While menopause can be challenging, it's also an opportunity to build a stronger, healthier relationship with yourself and those around you.

A thing learnt along the way

Find the source of your power

"Control the things you can control."
Samantha Stosur

Sometimes in life it can feel like things are happening to us. But the truth is that in any situation, we have power.

We just need to find the source of that power.

And that can be found in working out what it is that we can do.

Knowing what we can do allows us to have power in any situation.

The stuff that is out of our control - the things that we can't do anything about - is where we probably spend most of our time worrying. Which is futile.

Learning to accept the things we cannot do anything about, and identifying the things that we can, helps us to become more resilient and solution focused.

You need to slam a few doors
Suzanne Thompson

"You need to slam a few doors!" The examiner's verdict on my performance of a scene from Alice in Wonderland rings in my ears.

I am in junior school. I can see myself slowly, despondently returning to my classroom. I can smell custard drifting out from the dining hall. Why remember this scene so vividly? Why did that one phrase lodge so firmly in my mind?

At home no adult openly voiced their anger. Arguments were taboo, considered terminal, to be feared. Grandma if challenged, would huff and withdraw. Her noisy silence oppressive. It could last for days. Mum would go to bed. A closed door warned us off. Dad's anger occasionally escaped, but was almost immediately stubbed out.

From them I learned to suppress my anger. This has its benefits. Friends have told me I'm a good listener, able to see different sides of an argument, a reflector, a diplomat. I've been told I am easy to be with, personable, calm. It has allowed me to observe and to notice.

Yet, I wish I'd known that in suffocating my anger, I was losing something precious. A natural feeling to warn me that something might be harming me. By trying to keep the peace at all costs I ignored my needs and my wants. I'm now hunting, exploring, experimenting with this powerful feeling of anger. I now understand why I kept hold of the examiner's words.

When to apologise
Lisa Dymond

I don't know about you, but I wish I didn't feel the need to always apologise!

"I'm sorry for speaking my mind", "I'm sorry for telling the truth" or *conversely "I'm sorry for telling a white lie;" " I'm sorry if this offends you," "I'm sorry if I offend you". These* are some of the apologies that run through my mind, and thankfully less often now, out of my mouth.

To be able to write this down now and for some time before, I had really begun to notice myself doing this, or at least wanting to. Making any change, or carrying out any self-reflection, requires the acknowledgment of it, realising it and then practicing 'catching myself in the act' of doing it.

So why do it? Sometimes people *may* over-apologise as a trauma or a distress response, which can at times stem from a history of going to great lengths to avoid conflict. Sometimes a toxic or abusive relationship can elicit apologies because the thing is with people who have been or perceive themselves to have been hurt or humiliated often hope for or insist upon an apology. They (or we) may hope that by receiving an apology some dignity, trust, or a sense of justice will be restored with the acceptance of the wrongdoing. I will leave you to decide that one for yourself.

Sometimes guilty feelings or an assumption that something is wrong can be cause for an apology, sometimes rightfully, and sometimes unnecessarily. Again, I will leave you to decide that for yourself too.

So why do I do it?

I have come to understand that I am a people pleaser. I like to be nice, and kind and I like to be liked, or do I? I'm not obsequious, I am a genuine person and don't resort to flattery unless you deserve it, but I do like to please. Other people's happiness, pleasantness, or approval of me pleases me.

In **The Things I Wish I'd Known** *(2023)* my contribution was titled, *'I wish I'd known being me was actually, really okay'.* I discussed attachment and my own relationship with that. In summary, I gave a brief explanation in that as people we need to have strong emotional bonds and that strong emotional reactions can happen when these are threatened or broken and that this comes from our need for security and safety.

So, does low self-esteem cause unnecessary bursts of apologetic idiocy? Admittedly my need for security and safety includes an element of control, not to be controlling of or over others – that's something entirely different; but I do have a need to have control over how I am perceived and my desire for perfectionism. To be a fantastic mummy, a model wife, a faultless friend, a perfect person, and to excel professionally. And if I am all of these things to all of these people and if I please them in doing so, then my core belief is that I am safe and secure, my world is safe and secure.

Mmmm, ok well…… I don't see this as a personal flaw, however I have and do question and reflect on this core belief of mine, to keep it in check and it's always been an area of growth and development. I have to work at it.

Now, I mentioned kind and nice. I believe that as a girl and a woman this has been stereotyped into me. To be kind and nice is to be liked, to be accepted. And I am writing this from the perspective of a grown woman, for anyone else who feels that similar pressure.

Official definitions from vocabulary.com state that, *'to be nice is to be pleasant and good-natured. Polite people and sunny days are nice. Nice people and situations are enjoyable and don't cause problems. If you say something rude (or honest) to your sibling, your parents might say "Be nice!" The word is bland, a little vague and overused.'*

Do I want to be nice and avoid conflict? Yes of course I do, but not at the cost of being kind. These interchangeable words are frequently used hand in hand, and to be nice by my definition is, being polite, treating people well, being told to be nice, play nice and be pleasing. Whereas: *'The adjective kind also describes showing sympathy or giving comfort. If someone's feelings are hurt, a kind word can go a long way to making that person feel better'* (vocabulary.com). So, being kind is caring about someone, showing them you care, doing good things, and acting with kindness.

When thinking about being nice, I found myself scrolling the socials, have you seen the videos of people being 'nice' to others? I wonder perhaps if this is only to stage the video? How many hits? How many likes? From my viewpoint, it doesn't always feel genuine or sincere; to me it often seems as if it's only nice (*ick*) so that the content creator can get all the credit for themselves, for their own gain, and for a few more followers.

I reflect on my own people pleasing desires, if I am nice to another, I do have the expectations that they ought to behave nicely back and if they don't then my approval in their view doesn't seem validated, I'm not validated, I'm not valued. It's a disappointing truth and something that I have learned through acts and thoughts of kindness to myself not to dwell too much on.

So here's the difference. We have moved from being nice, to genuine and at times what can be difficult acts of kindness, which is a deliberate action, a behaviour, a choice and not for self-gratification, but building on firm foundations of integrity. As such saying 'no' might not seem the *nice* thing to do, but what if it is for a true act of *kind*ness or for another's benefit?

Back to conflict, usually seen as a negative interaction, but what about healthy conflict? This shouldn't be avoided and can be kinder: by inviting people to respectfully challenge you creates mutual empowerment, an understanding of each other and diverse opinions. Straight talking or telling the truth will involve giving people some form of feedback, even when it may involve having a difficult conversation and this should come from a place of support. This involves respect, builds on trust, strengthens our relationships and it will give you greater credibility.

Perhaps nice is a nice start and kindness requires growth?

Kindness takes strength and perhaps now we've wandered into asserting ourselves, protecting our boundaries and our values.

And then there's empathy, and practicing this rather than sympathy. It is largely acknowledged that empathy is shown in the compassion and understanding we can give to another. Sympathy on the other hand is pity. Empathy demonstrates the ability to understand how someone else feels while sympathy can be seen in the self-relief of not having the same problem or issues.

Perhaps empathy and kindness are related with having the emotional intelligence of understanding what another is feeling and being considerate to their needs creating a place of trust, safety, and security in our sincerity.

What have I learned? That by choosing my words differently, perhaps, and more often than not perhaps, just perhaps we do not need to apologise or even say sorry.

There will always be situations if when in the wrong an apology is absolutely necessary and totally called for, but if we are not in the wrong – why not ban Sorry! - or similar.

Don't excuse yourself or make excuses and become clever in an alternative rehearsed response, maybe saying 'thank you' fits instead of an apology. Maybe it doesn't. Perhaps offering support and showing that you care, or by pausing to choose our words with language that better and more accurately describes what is actually happening, shows our empathy and kindness in understanding.

Another way I am attempting to continue to condition my thinking and responses is to be more solution focused. It's still not always easy and I might feel like a situation, or event has in some way resulted in me feeling like it's all on me. That doesn't mean I have to apologise for it, and I can choose to be resilient and to think of a solution that works for me, that works for others and that works for the situation. Proposing a solution can be more powerful than an apology.

So how is this helpful? Is this helpful? Perhaps this has created more questions than answering the original question, or perhaps it was a statement: When to apologise - what is the thing I wish I'd have known?

I will probably always want to please people and be pleasing to them, but there's a better and kinder way to work with that, for all. I can admit and own my mistakes and I can apologise when I have done wrong, and I can choose my words wisely when I have not. I can choose to be honest and kind in the interactions I have with others, saying no when that is the kind thing to do and giving people the feedback and honesty they deserve from a place of mutual empowerment and of support.

Kindness, assertiveness, empathy, and confidence are key, they don't always come naturally, together, or straight away, so learn to fake it gracefully and unapologetically until you make it.

One of the things I wish I'd have known is when to apologise – which is when it's genuinely needed.

A thing learnt along the way

Leave some blank space

"Don't underestimate the power of Doing Nothing."
A.A. Milne

In the past, I have worn my ability to multi-task like a badge of honour. Why do one task when you can do two or three at once? Why leave any precious time unaccounted for during the day? I'm going to squeeze those 24 hours, 1,440 minutes, 86,400 seconds for everything I possibly can .

There is little blank space.

But it is so important to leave gaps in the day unfilled. Because we're not best served by always 'doing'.

Of course, the temptation to fill the gaps can be overwhelming – we are all so busy, after all. But stopping and embracing those pauses can be hugely beneficial, and significantly so for our wellbeing: letting those spaces be will actually make us feel better, and will allow us to be more effective.

Perhaps my daughter said it best when I mused on what task to do next recently when a gap in my day opened up.

Her advice?

"Rest."

If it matters to you, it matters
Hannah Freeman

It's taken me until my fourth decade, 25 plus years working, and being gifted the best job in the world – being mum to 10 and 13-year-old girls - to reflect, look back to my teenage years and really think about what it is I wish I'd known then.

And while we'll never have all - if any - of the right answers, my forty-something self thinks it might just boil down to this.

Get to know yourself better than anyone else. And if something truly matters to you, and makes your heart sing, it matters.

Trust yourself, trust your gut, and take time to stop, notice, and appreciate the parts of your life and those moments when you feel well and truly happy. Those moments might be a few short minutes in a day when a glimmer made you feel like yourself, or bigger chapters of your life when you felt content, calm, and happy. But whenever they occur, pay attention.

As you move through different stages of your life – at school, maybe college or university, as you form relationships, as you enter the world of work and maybe become a parent yourself, try and make it a habit to be present and consciously notice those happy moments when they happen. And as life gets busier and demands on you grow - don't lose sight of them along the way. Your happiness matters. Start now and your older 40-year-old self will thank you for it later.

Our teenage years, whatever generation we are born into, bring pressures, and life isn't one big happy collection of wonderful memories. As nice as that would be! At times, the expectations and messages about how you should look, behave, and live your life at times will be overwhelming. But never lose touch with who you really are. Please - forget about impressing or pleasing people or worrying about disappointing others. To my teenage self I'd say - keep true to you

And in the face of all these pressures, please never give up on doing the things that truly make your heart feel happy, and make you feel like you. Because that is the very best version of you.

And if you are lucky enough to find your 'thing' in your teenage years, hold on to it fiercely. Don't allow anything to prize it from your grasp.

Your happy 'thing' might be team sports, running, painting, poetry, getting lost in live music, dancing, reading, gymnastics, hiking, learning about the stars and planets, volunteering, or all of these things combined. Whatever it might be, when you find it, hold on to it tightly, and protect it fiercely because that – my girl - is what makes you, you.

And keep getting to know you. As the years fly by.

When you find and feel joy, pay attention.

When you notice you feel better and more positive and energised by people, spend more time with them.

When you laugh, like really belly laugh, look around and remember who you were with.

When you feel well, calm, and happy, notice your environment.

When you find something that makes your heart full, recognise it.

Because I really believe your heart and your gut will tell you everything you need to know.

Keep a diary, a journal, or a smile file. Store photos and clips from your favourite moments and memories in a separate album on your phone. And when you feel lost – return to these.

Reflect regularly about what has made you truly happy and keep pursuing more moments like those.

And know it's perfectly okay for these things to change and evolve, as you inevitably change too.

If something no longer brings you happiness, or you find new activities, people, and places that bring you more joy, run towards them. You can change, you can try new things, or drop something altogether. You get to decide. Know that it's okay to leave some things behind if the joy has fizzled out. There are no hard and fast rules here.

And guess what. You absolutely don't have to be brilliant at these things for them to matter.

You don't have to excel or even be averagely good at whatever it is that brings you joy, for it to do just that.

So what. You suck at singing, but it sets your soul alight. Join a choir anyway.

You were dreadful in your latest am dram performance, but the people you met were your tribe. Step onto that stage.

Your football team didn't win the league after all. But the girls had you belly laughing before and after every 90 minutes. Stick with them.

If 'your thing' brings smiles, laughter, makes you feel good, connects you with your people and adds a dose of sunshine, even on the greyest of days, then keep on doing it.

Because if it matters to you, it matters.

That's the lesson from the 'all grown up' 40 something version of me, and the message I'd like to pass on to my teenage self – a person that was trying to work out who she was back then.

Have the confidence and awareness to know yourself, and recognise all the things that make you, a happy you.

That's what I wish I'd known.

Navigating work and motherhood
Jana Patey

'I have time away from my kids, for my kids.
Because the time I pour into me, is what gives them
the better mum they deserve.
...My motherhood may not always look like yours.
But like yours, it's always all for my kids.'
(Emma Heaphy, Motherhood to Me, excerpts from a
poem '(Working) for them')

Today is Christmas Eve, it's early in the morning. The
house is quiet and dreamy. There is a glistening
Christmas tree next to me with the flickering lights
and festive cheer reflected in the tinsel woven in
between the green branches. We are at my mother-
in-law's house.

I have my traditional cookery book next to me, from
the country of my origin, trying to refresh my
memory with classic recipes close to my childhood.

Who is this all for?

For my children.

Showering them with traditions means working on
their festive spirit; making them feel the rhythm of
the year, reawakening their mixed identities and
honouring the richness of their cultural contexts.

My girls deserve the mountains of my effort, and every drop of sweat that comes out of me when rearranging my work to fit the holiday plans. When I'm exhausted above my laptop and the piles of books, I am still pressing on.

Motherhood is a wonderous and rewarding work that I treasure deeply. It is also very challenging and messy as expressed in the 'Motherhood to Me' piece by Emma Heaphy. No one can ever be the perfect mum.

I am a working mum. For most parts of my project and teaching work, I work from home. All the thinking and any quality work needs to be put in during the night-time hours.

Part of me needs to work for money, to live and to give. But beyond the tired narrative, in the nights when I lose myself in beautiful pieces of literature, I find the most powerful moments that feed my soul. Here, I find other puzzle pieces of me, and I am slowly crafting these into who I would like to become one day, as a professional and as a person.

I value my motherhood experience so much and I identify firstly as a mum. It will always be the most important part of me. But the work of motherhood can be combined with work on the self, professionally or personally. Instead of seeing my paid work as a barrier during my motherhood journey, I have reframed it as a valuable experience partly rooted in self-appreciation, curiosity, and inspiration. This chapter is a testimony of it. At present, I am a researcher and an academic. This line of work, as any, brings happy moments and low moments. But in this piece I want to recollect only the enriching moments, when my work had enabled me to seek new inspirations. This reframing has helped me to make sense of my dual experience. I believe it is helpful to see mothering and working as one blended experience rather than two opposites.

I have gradually come to realise that the large part of what I have been doing outside of mothering has encouraged me to embrace not only a growth mindset but also self-appreciation. Self-appreciation may seem a difficult concept to comprehend as a mother if you have been raised like me, in the world where mothers give their absolute selves to others, to the point of having nothing left of their own beings. The selfless love is an unimaginable part of motherhood and indeed very purposeful. But it is not the only type of love we can experience.

My mother identity and a working identity come strongly to the fore amongst the thousands of fragments of me. When it comes to the latter, I feel that I have come to appreciate how academia has shifted who I am. It has also affected what I am able to pass onto my girls because of my encounters with the most inspirational, strong, and courageous women. To some pursuing an academic identity might seem easy, or even pointless. What they don't realise is that academia is nothing but easy. It can feel very ruthless, it does ignite imposter syndrome more often than one would wish for, it can be overwhelming, causing exhaustion and frustration, and it is a precarious space full of inequalities and inherent opposing political forces. But for a long time it has also been a very special place that has fuelled me. Academia has enabled me to nurture my curiosity and through this, I feel I can go on and lead a more purposeful and fulfilled life. It has taught me to recognise and appreciate things I might have otherwise overlooked, through exposures to diverse insights, ideas, knowledge, and people I have met.

My paid work has given me a courage to embrace a more creative life. For example, it has fed my imagination, because I am lucky to be able to access the state of 'flow' through the reading and writing process (a term coined by Mihai Csikszentmihalyi). These are the moments where I am so deeply immersed in the work that the world around me stops and I feel purposeful, energized and happy. My work has opened my eyes and has taken me on paths underexplored. Research has enabled me to fight inequalities embedded in the systemic issues of oppressive workplaces, it has enabled me to be involved in some of the causes I believe in, it has taught me to be critical of status quo and has fuelled my desire to make an impact in the society, albeit in a small way.

My paid work has allowed me to lead a more inspired life. I am deeply appreciative of the strong and powerful women that I have met throughout my career, whether through their writings or personal interactions in academia and beyond. These encounters have enabled me to craft my sense of self that I believe would otherwise have remained dormant. In these spaces I have become more vulnerable and as a result, more accepting of myself, my successes as well as my failures.

My paid work has enabled me to cultivate an appreciation for novel sensory experiences, such as examining day to day working lives through arts-based research methods. Embracing aesthetics, I had been drawn recently to the work of an incredible artist Maria Eastwood. Maria lovingly created a series of angels on canvas with profound messages. I am a proud owner of one of these angels. The Angel of Self-Appreciation was created to accentuate the need for all women to pause in their daily pressure for perfection, triggered by society and social media, and internalised by many mothers. The angel symbolises the appreciation of who they are as women and what a great work they put in on their journeys. My angel radiates light and inspires me to recognise both beauty and darkness in humanity. In doing so, she reminds me to stay humble whilst nourishing my sense of self-worth. I find it not only through motherhood, but also through the enrichment moments my paid work gives me.

Professor Monika Kostera has reminded me of the importance to allow myself to be inspired not just by art and embedding art-based methods in academic expression. She teaches in *Occupy Management!* that because our day to day lives are 'managed' more than ever before, and we are required to do so much 'self-work' in the modern world, we may experience conditions of mastery but also despair and a senseless living. Professor Kostera underscores the open mindedness to get inspired by everyday encounters, spaces around us, by nature, pieces of writing and research and to be inspiring for others. Inspiration lead us to become better people, it stimulates 'empathy' and 'compassion' by enabling us to access our 'higher senses' or our 'higher functioning selves', as she points out. It is important to 'awaken[..] a desire to act on these aspects of the human psyche, to follow the impulses deriving from needs such as that of developing selfless relationships, of justice or of creating something new and original, and reflecting ideas acquired from excursions into the imaginative space.' (Kostera, 2014, p.30).

Research and academia has been an inspiration for me. They have challenged me and have led me to consider impact on society in the way I would not have been able to do within day-to-day organisational dogmas, tied to a working desk, feeling like 'a dead man working' (Cederström and Fleming, 2012) and caught up in the web of 'career ladders' and power struggles. Academia has not been a career ladder for me. Instead, it has given me freedom to think and courage to be creative.

I am a working mum, and I believe it is a hard balance to strike. I have part-time work, though at times it feels like a lot more. I work mostly from home. I set my boundaries around how I work, and I try hard to stick to them whenever possible. I practice saying 'no'. My work pace is slow but steady. I am not climbing any career ladder and that is ok. This is how I survive. But amongst the survival, there is joy.

I cherish the exposures my work has given me whilst on my motherhood journey. It has introduced me to the imaginative spaces, it has inspired me and it had exposed me to some of the most important questions in the 21st century, such as social relations, wellbeing, inclusion, and human rights.

So, what is it that I wish I'd known sooner?

I wish I'd realised a lot earlier how my work has helped me to stay open-minded, creative, inspired, vulnerable and imperfect, but most importantly – curious in everything and everyone around me. I wish that I hadn't tortured myself during my early motherhood journey on the balance between work and motherhood. I wish I realised sooner that my work hadn't limited me but it had helped me to be a stronger mum of my girls, more empowered and self-appreciative. I believe it has given me new strength to support them to live more informed, but also fruitful, joyous and purposeful lives.

This chapter is for my daughters, and other women who may recognise in themselves the struggle for balance between (self) work and motherhood.

Time is our most precious commodity
Katie Faulkner

In thinking about what to write for this piece, I was a bit stumped. I am not sure I have enough of life figured out to be able to impart sage wisdom to anyone really – and I certainly don't think that my answers would work for everyone.

But, in tried and tested fashion, when I asked the people that I would usually turn to with any sticky problem - my nearest and dearest - they gave me my answers. I'll share some of their thoughts on the following pages.

I was blown away by how similar the thoughts on this topic were from such a diverse group of people. We all wasted too much time worrying about other people's opinions when we were younger. Lots of us have been plagued with self-doubt or anxiety. None of us regretted investing in ourselves whether that was in respect of our health, finances or learning.

Talking to them helped me crystallize my own thoughts about what it would have been useful to know when I was younger. So, my learning (at the ripe old age of 41) is:

- Surround yourself with a tribe of amazing people, who will all have different life experiences, views, and ideas.

- Listen to them when they talk. And listen to understand rather than just waiting for your turn to speak.
- Recognise that some feedback or advice will work perfectly for you. Other bits you need to ignore and find your own way.

Crucially, I think my reflection on speaking to my friends is that time is our most precious commodity, and I wish I had known how it is in short supply by the time you hit your forties.

It is never a waste of time to spend it with family who make you feel safe and loved. A partner who is kind, and cares about your day. Spending time with friends who make your shoulders shake with laughter is the best medicine when you are feeling blue or harassed by the daily grind. Time spent watching your kids learn new things is both awe-inspiring and reminds you how much value there is in learning new things yourself. Travelling and keeping a sense of adventure keeps you feeling young and excited by life.

By our forties, most of us have realised that constant ecstatic happiness is not a baseline state at work, play, or home. The juggle to keep our lives in balance and everyone's needs serviced is tough. Moments of joy are to be treasured. Moments of pain will pass – with time (and wine). We have all experienced crushing grief of one type or another and know we will again. We are all getting older and aching a bit more. We are less perky (face, neck, boobs, spirit etc) but more reflective and grateful for what we have and who we have around us. And whilst I have this amazing group of people around me, I won't think too much more about what I wish I had known before, but I will focus on what they can keep teaching me for the next chunk of our lives together. Here are some of our shared thoughts, from my friends and I on what we wish we'd known:

1. **Stop worrying what other people think about you**
- Most people are as scared as you feel. No one knows what they are doing – they are probably just good performers and make it seem like they know.
- You are only really an extra in other people's lives. My twenties were an absolute mess. Glorious, chaotic, wine-soaked mess. But this was punctuated by worrying that everyone was dissecting my every word. I've learned that you are not the protagonist in everyone's story. You're a side character. So, if you say something cringe, no-one will remember or give it much thought. The reality is that people are too consumed in their own dramas, careers, relationships, their lives, to give your missteps more than a passing glance.

- I wish I had cared less about what people thought of me. Not tried so hard to please everyone because I realise that you just can't.
- Don't waste your time trying to be perfect and please everyone. Be awkward, be bold and make the mistake.
- Stop questioning who you are every time you make a tit of yourself.
- Make the choices and decisions based on what you want to do, not on what you think is expected of you or how you think you will be perceived.
- It's ok that some people are not for you. It is a waste of time to try and like them, or (worse) get them to like you.

2. There is no 'one-size fits all' career path
- Life is a marathon and not a sprint. Don't be in such a rush to do things and get places, it will come.
- Neither of my parents went to university. I was academic, but I didn't realise my options were broader than certain professions. I wish I'd known how many different ways there are to make a living – how many wonderful lives there are to live.
- It is ok to take a career break. Most people's careers take many forms over their lives with or without a career break. It is perfectly legit to take a break for your own health or to care for your children or your elders or just to

travel and have fun. You can come back to the working world as and when you want to and you can move to another career and try something else too. You can even do two or three things at once. Grab life with both hands and make brave choices that work for you.

3. **Don't let imposter syndrome or other people's expectations hold you back**
- When someone says you can't do something, know that what you believe you can achieve matters so much more than what someone else thinks you can. My A' level physics teachers told me I wouldn't be able to do an engineering degree. Well. I did.
- Be ambitious for yourself, don't stay in the holes people put you in.
- The things that make you different are the things that make you interesting. They are your Unique Selling Point. Value them and don't spend time trying to fit in or change them.

4. **Relationships – both romantic and friendships – should enhance your happiness**
- Hang out with people who make you feel loved rather than like you've 'made it'.
- Sometimes they are just not into you. You can't do anything to change it, doesn't mean that there is anything wrong with you or

indeed them – but once you have realised that it is actually very freeing.

- When you feel envy, use it as information for yourself rather than turning on the other person. That horrible feeling can help you see who you want to be and what you want for your own life.

5. Invest in yourself early, and often

- Embrace your freedoms when you are younger. Do the thing, spend the money, do as much as you can within your means.
- Do things that your future self will thank you for – so boring stuff like saving as soon as you practically can, but not completely at the expense of enjoying yourself.
- Wear SPF and start healthy habits for your physical and mental health – I don't think anyone who does those things regrets it.
- Not to rush. I was so focused on getting a job, getting a house, getting married that I didn't take opportunities when I had the chance. I wish I had taken a gap year, travelled and seen more of the world. I wish I had slowed down and made sure I was truly happy and not just box ticking.
- Most things feel less intense or better after a good night's sleep. Pause before you act.
- My anxiety increases when I am tired, or my brain is overloaded. I wish I'd known earlier

the importance of sleep and how it affects your brain.
- Be better when it comes to money and investing into my future and educate myself more on being smart with money.

6. Counting your blessings and not sweating the small stuff is as decent a path to happiness as any
- True happiness comes from recognising where and when you have been lucky – rather than assuming that you deserve 'it all' - and anything less than that feels like you are falling short.
- Comparison is the thief of joy. Aligning your expectations with your own reality makes feeling content easier.
- With kids – everything is a phase. Enjoy the good stuff. The bad stuff will pass.
- You don't have to react to everything in front of you. Doing or saying nothing is often the right thing to do.
- I didn't appreciate how many sacrifices my parents made for us. I had no idea the things that they did for us – we didn't have much money for expensive days out, but they made me realise that the fun free days are where the memories are made.

And, because she teaches me something every day, the last word goes to my eight-year old daughter, who once slipped this pearl of wisdom into a drawer at the Old Operating Theatre Museum in London Bridge when asked for her best piece of advice...

"Obsticals [sic] don't block the path, they are the path."

A thing learnt along the way

'There's time and then there's what you do with it.'

There's never enough time is there? The to do list always outweighs the amount of hours in the day. Running from one task to another, never stopping for breath, never pausing. Do, and do, and do again.

How often do we stop and think of what it is that we actually <u>want</u> to do?

I was reminded of this a few years ago when I was invited out to an event that sounded really fun. Yet I ummed and ahhed because of my teetering workload before saying "yes."'

On reflection, it struck me that this was exactly what I wanted to be doing with my time. And yet I also realised that so often we don't prioritise the stuff that really matters us.

I often have conversations with people about the things that are most important to us in our lives. But despite their significance to us, we devote such little time to these, put them at the bottom of our mental 'to do' lists. So often the things that we hold dear in our heart we completely overlook.

One thing I've learnt along the way is to remember it's ultimately up to me how I use this most precious commodity and so now I frequently stop and ask myself what it is that I want to be doing with my hours and days? And the answers I have found have been joyous, fulfilling, and completely worth the investment of my time.

Prioritise what matters to you
Georgina Phillips

At the time of writing this I am 43 years old. I've worked in the public relations industry for over 20 years and for the past 12, I've been the co-founder of healthcare PR agency Tonic Communications.

Nearly ten years ago I married a lovely, supportive man and in 2019 we welcomed our son.

As a professional I am proud of what I have achieved – I run a profitable, growing company alongside a business partner who I respect and love. And as we embark on another busy year, I reflect on the things that have changed me so much, and which really took me by surprise.

I wish I'd known how much my motivation for work would change over the years.

When I was at school, I remember vividly being sold the dream that us girls could 'have it all'. I come from a family of strong women who have always worked hard, and it spurred me on to be successful on my own merit. As money wasn't in abundance as a teenager, I worked for it – odd jobs spanning everything from shop work and babysitting to waitressing and factory work; I was motivated by money and the promise of it.

I have always been passionate and ambitious and a career in PR suited me down to the ground. While the industry held a certain glamour as I entered my first role straight from uni at 21, the speed and nature of each day continually proving my worth and fighting for results, and the client and peer schmoozing, was ideal. It might not have always felt like that at the time, but I recall it being fun and exciting during which I made some of the best friends of my life.

Working my way up the ranks I remember how I felt I needed to be aggressive to get where I wanted to be. Continually told by my (predominantly male) bosses to "better PR" myself and avoid being "overly emotional", I fought hard for a seat around the table. Throughout my twenties and into my early thirties, I moved around and worked with fantastic career-shaping brands, always working and playing hard.

Co-founding my own agency was always in my future. It felt so right, and I was never nervous about the risks – I just thought I'd always make it a success.

But that's where my naivety has really come to light.

For some reason I thought I would always be hungry to drive my career forward. And that, as I always joke – my agency would continue to be 'my first child'. But life happens, and priorities change.

I wish I'd known how difficult and emotionally draining the journey to becoming a mother was going to be and how different I would feel about work after having a child.

Mum guilt and the work-life juggle is tough, and I want to have quality time with my son while he's young. The flexibility of running my own agency means I can do that, which I am incredibly grateful for.

When I started my business, I wish I'd had more of a clear idea about what I wanted to get out of it and what the future should look like. Things like having a mentor, establishing a new business operation, setting a growth roadmap.

For the first five years of our business, we flew, and it seemed effortless - we were making money without really trying. And there was no real structure to how that happened. It was just lots of energy and passion and working really hard. That all changed with the arrival of children and then Covid, plus just getting older and seeing our priorities shifting.

I wish that the whole women can 'have it all' promise wasn't so prevalent, because it's impossible to aspire to. It's an unhealthy narrative. It's important instead to decide what you should and want to focus on and be true to yourself in making that a priority.

Finally, I wish I'd known to listen and follow my instincts more – intuition is an invaluable gift, and I now allow it to lead a lot more decisions.

Don't ignore what burns inside
Michelle Gant

I published my first book when I was seven years old.

'John, Claire, and Ann' recounted the adventures of three children who happened to very closely resemble me and my friends who lived next door, our identities cleverly disguised through use of our middle names. Not only did I write the story, I illustrated it, and self-published it too, aided only by felt tip pens, a pair of scissors, and a stapler.

I am pleased to say it was a massive hit with readers (my mum and dad) and so, buoyed by their enthusiasm and praise, I quickly (the next day I think) produced the sequel.

At seven years old I knew that this was my thing. I loved it. So much so that aged ten at primary school, I re-entered the world of publishing, creating a school magazine called *Eyecatchers*. To begin with, before fellow pupils came on board, it was just me on my own in my bedroom, writing and drawing (which I have to say, I am very much not adept at. But I didn't let that stop me). A key feature of the magazine was the song lyrics that, in the days pre-Google, required me to write down verbatim what I had heard on the radio - which in those heady eighties days of big ballads and rock songs, I didn't always get right. (Still, I never had any complaints).

I carried on writing throughout my teenage years, mostly in my diaries. I kept a journal for many years, a space to record my angst; as my little sisters found out – much to their hilarity - when they got caught reading one. They received a telling off from my parents who recognised that my diaries were sacrosanct. (Nicky and Jo, I forgive you!)

When it came to choosing a career, there was only one condition I had – it had to involve writing. Happily the path I have chosen has meant that I get to write every day in a whole myriad of different ways. I feel very lucky that I get to do what I do for a living.

But, as I entered my twenties and thirties, my creative writing petered out. Every now and then, I would feel the passion burn inside me to create a story or a poem and I would throw myself upon my computer, the words fizzing out of me. Only, these were never for sharing. Because by then, I had lost confidence. I felt far too shy and scared to ever share my writing with the world, to the point that if my partner latterly my husband ever walked in the room whilst I had a document I was working on open, I would shout at him to get out and hastily shut it down.

When my daughter was born, however, two things happened. The first was that her arrival reignited the writing spark inside me and I found the words tumbling out of me. I could not stop; I felt absolutely compelled to write, write, write. In between feeds, in the morning before she roused, in the early hours when she woke, tapping out notes on my phone. Prose, poetry, and a fictional blog inspired by my experiences of being a mum. Told through the voice of Baby Anon, the blog took a whimsical, humorous view of her parents' parenting wins and fails. It made me laugh, it offered me a different perspective on my worries and anxieties, and I think it was absolutely a crucial component in managing my mental health in the early days of motherhood.

The second thing that happened around this time was I realised that I was no longer too shy to share my words. I was starting to feel like a writer, and a writer who wanted people to read what I wrote. That's not to say I wasn't absolutely terrified the first time I shared a Baby Anon blog post on my private Facebook page (I turned my phone off for the evening in anticipation of the negative feedback which never came).

After the first time I shared something I had written, it got easier and easier. And so I wrote. And I published my words. Essays I wrote ended up on news and blogging and parenting sites (and some American organisations actually paid me for my reflections. Who would have thought it!?) I carried on writing my Secret Life of the Baby blog, setting up a whole social media presence for Baby Anon, eventually turning the blog into a book which I self-published. And my poems, well, I am perhaps proudest of all that they have been read at some of the happiest and the saddest family occasions.

The arrival of the pandemic caused me once again to find solace and succour in writing. With a difference. I decided to keep a diary about that time. Which became an online blog with a different contributor every day. In the end some 75 people of all ages and from different places took part – and we had this amazing book, When The World Paused. This was sold to raise money for NHS charities. That wasn't the end of it though and I repeated the whole process again the following year with When The World Paused: What A Pandemic Taught Us About Living. This time 84 people took part, including a number of people who had shared their stories the first time round, writing about how life had moved on. Once again, we had this incredible book which I published for NHS Charities. The response was amazing, and in fact, there is a recording of my daughter and I reading her reflections – which I'd written from what she told me verbatim as she was just four at the time – as part of the British Library's Covid Collection.

I loved it. I loved bringing people together to share words and make books for good. Which brought me to the first The Things I Wish I'd Known in 2023, which I adored so much. And now, you find me here, at the end of More Things I Wish I'd Known. I really hope that you have enjoyed reading the essays in this book as much as I did, from the very first time I received them.

And so, there are three things I think I've learnt above all else through my relationship with writing:

- If there is a dream that burns inside you, don't ignore it. If you have a purpose, a passion, an ambition that refuses to be ignored – don't. Let it out. Even if you're not sure if you're good enough. Even if you're scared. Accept it and allow it to unravel - who knows where it might take you.

- *"It is never too late to become what we might have been."* I love this quote from George Eliot. I am 50 next year and I feel like I am just getting started with writing and books, and sharing stories. I can't imagine not doing this. There'll be more, more, more - prose and poems and fiction and I heartily hope non-fiction like this. It makes my heart sing.

- Writing is so powerful. Throughout my life, from my teenage diaries to my Baby Anon blog to the books during Covid to now, writing has been cathartic for me. It has set me free when I've been stuck, it has offered me a different perspective, and it has provided me a conduit to express myself at the best times, the worst times, and all the times in between. (Full disclosure, I have found writing my essays in this book emotional. In a very good way.) I know too that many of the wonderful women involved in this collection of reflections have found the act of writing similarly helpful, moving, and inspiring.

So that's all from us, and now it's over to you. You'll find pages at the end of this book where you can write down whatever thoughts you want to get out on paper.

Thank you so much for reading.

A thing learnt along the way

Choose your own story

"You can't go back and change the beginning, but you can start where you are and change the ending."
C S Lewis.

When I was a child, the choose your own ending books were popular. I was the proud owner of several of these type of books, and I would love reading them again and again, selecting a different story route if I didn't like the way one narrative had ended.

Unfortunately life isn't like that. We don't have the opportunity to restart, to revisit our younger selves and try something new.

But what we do have is the opportunity to start again, right where we stand. And we don't need a trigger to do so - a new year, or a milestone birthday, or anything else that can provide an external catalyst for change.

Whenever we want, however we want, we can write a different storyline for ourselves.

It's all within our power.

References

46: Squiggly Careers podcast. www.amazingif.com

90: Tolle, Eckhart: The Power of Now – published 1997

99, 103: McCall, Davina and Potter, Dr Naomi: Menopausing: The Positive RoadMap to Your Second Spring – published 2022

99, 103: The Dr Louise Newson Podcast

103: Casperson, Kelly: You Are Not Broken – published 2024

109: Gant, Michelle and various contributors: 'The Things I Wish I'd Known' – published 2023

123, 124: Heaphy, Emma: Motherhood and Me – published 2021

126: Csikszentmihalyi, M. (2002) Flow: The Classic Work on How to Achieve Happiness. London: Rider

127: Eastwood, M. Artwork Angel of Self-appreciation. www.sacredsoulscapes.com/angel/

128: Kostera, Monica: Occupy Management – published 2015

129: Cederström, C. and Fleming, P. (2012) Dead Man Working. Winchester: Zero Books.

Keep in touch

We'd love to hear from you.

Please do get in touch with your thoughts on the book, and we'd also love to hear from you if you'd like to take part in future collections.

We are **engaging stories** on Facebook and LinkedIn, and you can email us engagingstories@yahoo.com

Your space
This is your space.

Please use it to capture any reflections on the things you've read in this book, set out any goals, write down any things you're grateful for, or scribble any thoughts that you want to get out on paper.

Printed in Great Britain
by Amazon